H.G. Wells

The Time Machine

Adaptation and activities by **Derek Sellen**
Illustrated by **Paolo D'altan**

© 2018 D Scuola SpA
Via Privata Mondadori, 1 – 20054 Segrate (MI)
First edition: January 2018

We would be happy to give you further information concerning our material and receive your comments.

info@blackcat-cideb.com
blackcat-cideb.com

Content editor: Maria Grazia Donati
Editor: Francesca Pinagli
Design: Sara Fabbri, Erika Barabino
Page Layout: Annalisa Possenti
Picture research: Alice Graziotin

Art Director: Nadia Maestri

DEALINK, DEAFLIX are trademarks licensed by De Agostini SpA

Picture credits:
Shutterstock; iStockphoto; Culture Club/Getty Images: 4; Ann Cutting/Photolibrary/Getty Images: 38; COLLECTION CHRISTOPHEL/MONDADORI PORTFOLIO:83, 108, 109

All rights reserved. No part of this book may be reproduced, stored in a retrieval system or transmitted, in any form of by any means, electronic, mechanical, photocopying, recording or otherwise, without the written permission of the publisher.

Member of CISQ Federation

CERTIFIED MANAGEMENT SYSTEM
ISO 9001

The design, production and distribution of educational materials for the CIDEB (Black Cat) brand are managed in compliance with the rules of Quality Management System which fulfils the requirements of the standard ISO 9001

Reprints
10 9   8   7   6   5   4   3   2   1
2031 2030 2029 2028 2027 2025

Printed in Italy by Italgrafica srl – Novara

Contents

CHAPTER 1	***The fourth dimension***	8
CHAPTER 2	***Into the future***	18
CHAPTER 3	***The disappearance***	29
CHAPTER 4	***Weena***	42
CHAPTER 5	***Two worlds***	52
CHAPTER 6	***Escape from the Morlocks***	63
CHAPTER 7	***The journey to the Porcelain Palace***	73
CHAPTER 8	***Fire!***	87
CHAPTER 9	***The journey continues***	98

DOSSIERS	H.G. Wells	4
	A short history of science fiction	38
	Is time travel possible?	83
	Cinema: *The Time Machine*	108

ACTIVITIES	Before you read	7, 17, 28, 41, 51, 62, 72, 86, 97
	The text and beyond	14, 25, 35, 48, 59, 69, 80, 94, 105
	After reading	110

PRELIMINARY This icon indicates Preliminary-style activities

T: GRADE 6 This icon indicates Trinity-style activities

  THE STORY IS FULLY RECORDED.

H.G. Wells

Herbert George Wells was born in 1866 in Bromley, just outside London, in the south-east of England. His family were not rich. His father was a small shopkeeper and his mother had been a servant. When Wells broke his leg as a child, he began to read while he was recovering. He found that he loved books.

His father's business could not support the family. So in 1880, Wells had to start work in a shop as an apprentice.[1] He worked for thirteen hours each day and slept in one big bedroom with other apprentices. His mother returned to work as a servant in a large house. When Wells visited her, he was able to read in the library there and to develop his experience of literature.

He managed to escape from the hard life of a shop apprentice and, little by little, he gained educational qualifications while working as a teacher. Life was never easy for him and he later wrote that he was often hungry. However, he eventually gained a university degree. In fact, his first published work was not a novel, but a school book about biology.

His real ambition was to be a writer of fiction and of social studies. Many of his early novels were 'scientific romances'. These included *The Island of Doctor Moreau*, *The Invisible Man*, *The War of the Worlds* and *The First Men in the Moon*. They are still popular today. The first of these was published in 1895. It was *The Time Machine*.

---

1. **apprentice** : someone who is learning how to work in a job.

H.G. Wells wrote many other types of book. His best-known novels include *Kipps*, which is about a young man who suddenly becomes rich. The book shows Wells's interest in class differences in Britain. The musical and film *Half a Sixpence* were based on *Kipps*. He also wrote non-fiction books about western society and about his ideas of how the world would develop in the future.

In the 1930s, he predicted the Second World War and the terrible effects of bombing from the air. He thought that the only solution to the political chaos and conflict in the world was a world government. He also wanted to establish a 'World Encyclopaedia' which would grow and change over time. It should be open to every person in the world. But Wells died in 1946, long before his dream became reality through the Internet and Wikipedia.

Wells wrote more than 110 books, including 50 novels. He continues to be regarded as a controversial[2] and influential thinker as well as the author of long-lasting stories about the possibilities of science and about the lives of the various unforgettable characters that he invents.

Comprehension check

1 Now answer these questions. Include some information to support your answers.

1 When and why did H.G. Wells first become interested in reading?
2 Did Wells's education finish after he started work as an apprentice?
3 What advantage did his mother's job have for him?
4 Was *The Time Machine* his first published book?
5 Did Wells want to write fantasy novels about imaginary worlds?
6 Did some of his predictions about the future come true?

---

2. **controversial** : having opinions which divide people or make people angry.

The characters

From left to right:
Narrator, Time Traveller, Weena, an Eloi, a Morlock

ACTIVITIES

Before you read

Use a dictionary if necessary to help you complete these activities. You will meet these words as you read Chapter 1.

Geometry

1 Complete the notes with the words in the box.

> cube   geometry   line   plane   rectangle   triangle
> three-dimensional   two-dimensional   two-dimensional

> Today, we studied (1) .... :
> A (2) .... is one-dimensional. A (3) ....
> has three sides. It is (4) .... A (5) ....
> has four sides. It is also (6) .... A solid with six
> square faces is a (7) .... It is (8) ....
> A (9) .... is a flat surface.

Jobs

2 Read about four people with certain jobs. Fill the gaps by choosing four words from the box.

> director   editor   journalist   mayor   psychologist   teacher

1 The .... is planning to create a new park in the town.
2 Amy is a .... She writes about the news.
3 Bill is the .... of the newspaper, so he makes the final decisions.
4 Jane is a .... She wrote a book called *The Mind*.

7

CHAPTER 1

The fourth dimension

The Time Traveller was talking to us about Space and Time. His grey eyes shone and his face was lively. I have called him the 'Time Traveller' even though at this moment we didn't know about his invention. He had invited us to his house. After dinner, we sat comfortably beside a warm fire and relaxed.

'You must listen carefully,' he said. 'I am going to disagree with some ideas which you all believe. For example, the geometry which you studied at school is wrong!'

There were six of us in his audience: a friend called Filby, a psychologist, a local mayor, a young man, a doctor and myself. We had no idea that we would hear a story which few of us would believe. We would see strange, impossible things.

'I shall give you reasons for everything that I say. You know that a line in mathematics does not exist in reality. It has zero

The fourth dimension

thickness. A plane also has no existence. They are just abstract ideas.'

'Yes,' agreed the psychologist.

'And a cube does not exist in reality,' continued the Time Traveller.

'Nonsense,' said Filby. 'Of course a cube exists. It's a solid.'

'No, a three-dimensional geometrical cube is just an idea. If a cube existed in reality, it would have four dimensions — length, width, height and duration.[1] In other words, it must exist in Space and Time. There are really four dimensions: three of Space and one of Time. We often forget this.'

The Time Traveller continued to explain that people often have the wrong idea about 'the Fourth Dimension'.

'The "Fourth Dimension" is not Space, but Time.'

The poor mayor repeated the strange words 'fourth dimension' quietly to himself, without understanding.

'There may be many pictures of the same man at different moments in Time,' said the Time Traveller. 'Here he is at eight years old, at fifteen, another at seventeen, another at twenty-three, and so on. The man is three-dimensional but he also exists in Time. His being is four-dimensional.'

'But if Time is a fourth dimension of Space,' asked the doctor, 'why can't we move about in Time in the same way as we move in Space?'

'We can only move forwards and backwards in Space. We need a machine to move up and down, a hot-air balloon[2] for example.'

'But we cannot move at all in Time,' argued the doctor.

---

1. **duration**: the quality of existing in Time.
2. **hot-air balloon**:

CHAPTER **1**

'Yes, we can. We move along the Time-Dimension at the same speed from the cradle [3] to the grave.'

'But we cannot travel backwards in Time,' said the psychologist.

'We can travel back in our imaginations. We cannot stay there for long. But we can use a machine, the balloon, to travel up and down in Space. So perhaps we can invent a machine that helps us to travel in Time!'

The Time Traveller continued confidently. 'For a long time I've thought about inventing a machine like this, which I can drive in any direction in Space *and* Time. And now I have proof!'

'We could go back to the time of famous events so that we can see if history is correct,' suggested the psychologist.

'We might talk to the Ancient Greeks and hear Homer and Plato,' said the young man. 'Or even go into the future.'

'We might discover a perfect future society,' I said, 'a society where everyone is equal. The future must be better.'

'It's a mad idea,' said the psychologist.

'Do you really have proof?' I asked with excitement.

The Time Traveller smiled. He went out of the room and down the long corridor towards his laboratory. The psychologist looked at us. 'I wonder what he will show us.'

When the Time Traveller returned, he held in his hand a shining metallic framework, the size of a small clock. It was beautifully made. There was ivory [4] and a crystalline material in it. He placed the tiny machine on one of the small tables in the room. There was a bright lamp on the table and several candles in the room. We could all see clearly. It wasn't a trick. That's impossible.

---

3. **cradle** : a baby's small bed. 'From the cradle to the grave' means from birth to death.
4. **ivory** : material from an elephant's tusk/tooth.

The fourth dimension

'Well?' said the psychologist.

'This is only a model,' said the Time Traveller. 'It is my plan for travelling through Time. You can see that it seems unreal. It twinkles.[5] Here is one little white lever and here is another.' We all looked closely at the mysterious object.

'It took two years to make. This lever sends the machine into the future. And this other lever sends it into the past. The traveller sits here on this seat. I am going to press the lever in a moment and the machine will disappear.'

There was a pause.

He moved his finger towards the lever. 'No, wait,' he said, and took the psychologist's hand in his. The psychologist pressed the lever with his finger.

There was a light wind in the room. One of the candles blew out. The little machine turned round and became faint. It seemed like a ghost of itself. Then it disappeared completely.

We looked at each other silently. 'Are you serious?' asked the doctor. 'Do you think that the machine is in the future?'

'Yes, I do. Also, I am building a big Time Machine in my laboratory. It is nearly finished. I am planning to go on a journey into the future myself.'

We sat and looked at the empty table. We were amazed.

'Would you like to see the Time Machine itself?' The Time Traveller led us down the corridor to his laboratory. There, we saw a much larger machine, similar to the little object we had seen but big enough for a man to sit inside. It was made of nickel, ivory and crystalline rock. It was almost complete, but twisted crystalline bars lay on the floor next to it with some complicated drawings.

---

5. **twinkle** : shine with an irregular light.

CHAPTER 1

'Are you serious?' asked the doctor.

'I am going to explore Time. Yes, I am serious.'

A little later, we all left. Was it a trick? Can human beings really travel into the past or the future?

The next Thursday I returned to the Time Traveller's house. Some other guests were already there, including the doctor. How had he made the small model of the machine disappear?

We waited in the same room. The psychologist was there. In addition, there was the editor of a newspaper, a journalist and a quiet shy man.

'It's half-past seven,' the doctor said, 'We ought to have dinner.'

I asked where the Time Traveller was.

'Nobody knows.'

Then the door from the corridor opened slowly and silently.

The Time Traveller appeared.

'Good heavens! What's the matter with you?' asked the doctor.

Everyone turned towards the door. The Time Traveller was in a terrible condition. His coat was dirty. His hair was very untidy and it seemed to be greyer than before. His face was pale. There was a cut on his chin. He looked extremely tired. For a moment, he stood in the doorway. Then he came into the room. He was limping.[6]

He said nothing but asked to drink something. We all waited for him to speak.

---

6. **limp** : walk with difficulty, e.g. because of an injury.

ACTIVITIES

The text and *beyond*

Comprehension check

1 For each sentence answer (T) True or (F) False.

		T	F
1	The Time Traveller is called Filby.	☐	☐
2	The Time Traveller believes that there are four dimensions.	☐	☐
3	The Traveller has invented a hot-air balloon that can travel in Time.	☐	☐
4	The Traveller shows his guests the small Time Machine.	☐	☐
5	At the time that they leave the Traveller's house, all the men believe in 'time travel'.	☐	☐
6	When the person who is telling the story returns to the Time Traveller's home, the Traveller is not there.	☐	☐
7	The same people are at the house on each occasion.	☐	☐
8	When the Traveller appeared, he seemed to be tired and dirty.	☐	☐

… we didn't know about his invention. He had invited us to his house.

Look at these events and when they happened.
 1 He invited us to his house.
 2 The Time Traveller explained his ideas.

We use the past perfect simple form of the verb (**had** + past participle) to show that one action happened earlier than another action in the past.

The Time Traveller explained his ideas. He **had invited** us to his house.

Grammar: writing about the past

2 Look at the sentences (1-5). Which event happened first? Which event happened second? Rewrite the sentences with one verb in the past simple and one verb in the past perfect simple.

   0 He (*show*) us a small machine which he (*make*) earlier.
      He **showed** us a small machine which he **had made** earlier.

14

ACTIVITIES

1. He (*talk*) about the geometry that we (*learn*) at school.
2. I (*begin*) to believe in time travel after I (*see*) the machine.
3. I (*go*) back to his house. The others (*arrive*) before me.
4. After we (*start*) dinner, the Traveller (*return*).
5. He (*come*) into the room. Perhaps he (*travel*) into the future and back.

Interpretation

3 What is the Time Traveller like? Which statements below do you agree with? Why?

- highly intelligent
- wants to trick other people
- serious and confident
- enjoys explaining his ideas
- knows how to develop his invention quickly
- brave
- more interested in the past than in the future
- adventurous

4 Here are some opinions about Chapter 1. Do you agree or disagree? Give each opinion a score:

5 = strongly agree   4 = agree   3 = perhaps agree
2 = disagree   1 = strongly disagree

Compare and discuss your ideas with another student's.

1. This story starts very slowly. I want more excitement. ☐
2. I find the ideas about Time and Space very interesting. ☐
3. It is easy for the reader to imagine the people and the events. ☐
4. There are too many unimportant characters. ☐
5. This beginning makes me want to read more. ☐
6. I like the style of writing. ☐
7. It is very different from a modern story about time travel. ☐
8. The story is improbable. ☐

ACTIVITIES

Comprehension

5 PRELIMINARY Look at the text in each box. What does it say? Mark the correct letter: a, b or c.

FUTURA TRAVEL
Visit the future!
- Travel by super-fast coaches
- Stay in luxury hi-tech hotels
- Go to amazing locations

You'll imagine you're in the 22nd century!

1. This advert is for:
   a ☐ time travel into the future.
   b ☐ high-quality holidays in the present.
   c ☐ an exhibition about the future.

MISSING

Professor Amis has disappeared.

Last seen two weeks ago on Monday 27th June at the University Laboratory where he carries out research into the possibilities of time travel.

2. Professor Amis:
   a ☐ is a scientific researcher.
   b ☐ is a time traveller.
   c ☐ has been missing since last Monday.

LOST IN GALAXY X31

A film about a 100-year journey through space to an unknown star system.
See the monsters of another world and the bodies of lost astronauts floating in Space.
Not suitable for children under 10.

3.
   a ☐ This is probably a horror film.
   b ☐ No children should see this film.
   c ☐ It is a film about time travel.

Is Time Travel Possible?

Doctor Clarke, the writer of *Journeys through Time* and other books about the science of time travel, will give a talk on Friday in the library.

Buy tickets online for this event.

Open to the public as well as students.

4.
   a ☐ Doctor Clarke writes stories about time travel.
   b ☐ You can buy his book online.
   c ☐ Anyone can attend this event.

ACTIVITIES

Before you read

Predicting the story

1 What problems may you find if you travel through Time to meet the people of the future?

- language
- advanced science
- super intelligence
- new ways of communicating
- different ideas about life
- illness

Discuss these and further possible problems with other students.

Materials

2 Match the descriptions (1-5) with the materials (a-e).

1 ☐ This material is often used for statues in the street.
2 ☐ This comes from elephants. Nowadays, it is not legal to obtain it.
3 ☐ This is a bright reddish-brown metal. It sometimes becomes green in colour.
4 ☐ This expensive material is used for statues, tables, churches, etc. One of the most famous and best types comes from Carrara, Italy.
5 ☐ This is a fine material which is used for cups and plates.

a ivory
b marble
c copper
d porcelain
e bronze

Vocabulary

3 Here are some words you will meet in Chapter 2. Look up any unknown words or ask other students.

1 bushes
2 lawn
3 Sphinx
4 tunic
5 hail

17

CHAPTER **2**

Into the future

The Time Traveller looked at us all. He seemed to be waking up from a dream.

'I'm all right.' His eyes became brighter and his cheeks were less pale. 'I'm going to wash and put on clean clothes. Save me some food. I'm extremely hungry and I want meat!'

He left the room. I saw that his feet were blood-stained. The editor said, 'Extraordinary behaviour[1] of a famous scientist.' It sounded like the headline for an article in his newspaper.

'I'm sure it's connected with time travel,' I said. The editor and the journalist laughed. For them, it was a stupid idea.

The Time Traveller came back and joined us. He was dressed in clean clothes but his face was still tired.

---

1. **behaviour** : way of doing things.

Into the future

'These people have told me that you travelled into the middle of next week,' joked the editor. 'Can you tell us the name of the winning horses in the races?'

The Time Traveller didn't answer but smiled and started eating.

'Give us your story! Have you travelled in Time?'

'Pass the salt,' said the Time Traveller, refusing to answer until he had eaten. We all wanted to ask questions but we had to wait.

At last, the time Traveller pushed away his plate. 'I've had an amazing time,' he said. 'I've been to the future.'

'It's impossible to travel in Time,' said the editor.

'I'm too tired to argue,' he replied. 'I will tell you the story of my journey. But please don't interrupt. You will think that I am lying. But it's all true. I was in my laboratory at four o'clock today and since then I've lived eight days! Eight wonderful days, eight terrible days! I'm very tired but I must tell you about it. Then I shall go to bed. But please, no interruptions.'

'We agree.'

The Time Traveller began his story. He spoke like a very tired man. Later, he became livelier. We sat in the darkness while the lamp lit his white, sincere face. At first, we looked at each other but soon we concentrated only on the Time Traveller.

This is his story in his own words.

* * *

'I showed some of you the Time Machine last week. The machine was complete this morning. At ten o'clock, I tested everything for the last time, put one more drop of oil on it and sat on the seat. I took the starting lever in one hand and the stopping lever in the other. I started it and almost immediately stopped it. I seemed to fall for a second. I felt sick. That was all. I looked at the laboratory around me. Everything looked the same.

CHAPTER 2

But the clock told me a different story. I had started the machine at about one minute past ten. Now it was nearly half-past three!

I breathed deeply and grasped the starting lever with both hands. The journey into the future started. The laboratory became misty and then dark. My housekeeper,[2] Mrs Watchett, walked slowly across the room. She didn't see me. To me, she seemed to pass like a rocket! I moved the lever to its maximum position. Night came. A moment later, it was morning. The laboratory became more and more unclear. Tomorrow night came, then day again, then night again, day again, faster and faster. A sound filled my ears.

It is impossible to really describe the feeling of time-travelling. It is not pleasant. I travelled forward in Time helplessly, afraid that I was going to crash into something. As my speed increased, night followed day like the moving of a black wing. The laboratory disappeared and I saw the sun as it ran across the sky. My eyes hurt. The moon was going through its quarters from new to full and the stars circled. Gradually, night and day mixed and I saw only an overall greyness. The sun was a streak[3] of fire and the moon a silver band.

Of course, I was still in the same place, the hill on which this house stands. Trees changed from green to brown to black. I saw huge buildings appear and disappear as they were built and then knocked down. The seasons passed from snow to green to grey to snow again. I looked at the dials of the machine and realised that my speed was more than one year in a minute.

I began to feel more comfortable. The machine moved strangely but I felt extremely happy. I threw myself into the future. I began to wonder about this future. What wonderful developments were

---

2. **housekeeper**: someone who is paid to clean the house, cook, etc.
3. **streak**: a fast-moving, long, thin shape.

Into the future

happening all around me as I travelled? What fantastic advances were human beings making? I saw tall buildings in the mist. I saw a rich green countryside. The world seemed very beautiful.

I decided that I had to stop. But I knew that I might crash into a building or a tree. As I travelled through Time, this was not a problem. I slipped through Space like a thin gas. But when I stopped, the machine might explode if it hit something.

When I was at home in my laboratory, I accepted the danger. But now it was real. The Time Machine moved like a ship rolling on the sea and I felt sick. I decided to stop immediately. The dials on the Time Machine had told me that I had reached the year 802701. I pulled the stop lever sharply and the machine turned over.

It threw me through the air. There was a great thunder in my ears. I was sitting on grass in front of the machine. It was hailing. Slowly, things became clear. I was on a small lawn in a garden, surrounded by flowering bushes. Their purple and pink flowers fell as the hail hit them. In a few moments, I became very wet. "This is fine weather to greet a man who has travelled thousands of years to see you," I thought.

I stood up. Beyond the bushes, there was a huge white figure made of stone. As the hail cleared, I saw it more clearly. It was very big, far taller than the tree next to it. It was made of white marble and looked like a sphinx with wings. It was on a large bronze base. The eyes of the stone face seemed to watch me and there was the shadow of a smile on the lips. As I looked at this mysterious creature, the hail stopped.

I asked myself questions. "Would the future people see me as a dirty horrible animal that they would immediately kill?"

I could see other buildings in the distance. I was afraid and turned back to the Time Machine. As I did so, the sun came out

CHAPTER 2

and the sky became an intense blue. My courage returned. I saw a circular window in the wall of one of the buildings. A group of figures stood watching me. They were wearing rich soft clothes.

Then I heard voices. Men were running through the bushes towards me. One of them emerged in front of me. He was a small creature — much shorter than I am — and wore a purple tunic[4] with a leather belt. He had bare legs and sandals on his feet and no hat. I noticed for the first time that the day was very warm. He was a beautiful and graceful creature, but very fragile. He seemed almost like a sick person with a fever.

A moment later, we stood face to face. He came straight up to me and laughed. He had no fear. Then he turned to his two companions and spoke to them in a strange sweet-sounding language.

Others arrived until there was a group of about ten. One of them spoke. He came forward, paused and then touched my hand. Then I felt other soft fingers on my back and shoulders. They wanted to make sure that I was real. I was not scared. These pretty little people seemed harmless and, anyway, they seemed so weak that I was sure I could fight them. They were gentle and childlike.

They began to feel the Time Machine. At once, I warned them not to touch it. I removed the stop and start levers and put them in my pocket. I studied them. Their hair was curly and came to a sharp end at their necks and cheeks. There was no hair on these men's faces. Their mouths were small with bright red lips and they had little pointed chins.[5] Their eyes were large and gentle. They stood there smiling and making soft noises to each other.

---

4. **tunic**: a piece of clothing that covers the body from the neck to the knees; it was worn by men in ancient times.

5. **pointed chins**:

CHAPTER 2

I pointed to the Time Machine and myself. Then, trying to express the idea of Time, I pointed to the sun. At once, one of the creatures copied me and made the sound of thunder. He was using sounds and gestures[6] to ask me: did you come from the sun in a thunderstorm?

I was very surprised. Were these creatures fools? I had always expected that the people of the future would have far greater knowledge than we have. I expected them to know all about science and nature. But this question showed that they were like five-year-old children. I was greatly disappointed.

Had I built the Time Machine and come face to face with danger just to meet these pretty child-men?

I pointed to the sun again and made the sound of thunder. They stepped back from me and bowed.[7] Then one placed a chain of beautiful flowers over my head. The others clapped and, laughing, threw more flowers at me. Then they led me towards the nearest building. I thought about my idea of highly intelligent super-men and super-women of the future and laughed at my own stupidity.

---

6. **gestures** : movements with the hands and arms.
7. **bow** : show respect, e.g. for a king, by bending the body from the waist.

ACTIVITIES

The text and *beyond*

Comprehension check

1 Give brief answers to these questions about Chapter 2.

1. Why did the men have to wait for the Time Traveller to begin to answer their questions?
2. How long had the Time Traveller been away?
3. How did he feel during the first part of his journey through Time?
4. What kind of buildings and people did he expect to find?
5. Was it dangerous to stop the Time Machine?
6. What strange object did he see when he landed?
7. Why wasn't he afraid of the people of the future?
8. When he pointed to the sun, what did the little people think?

Interpretation and Internet research

2 Wells wrote this story in 1895. Answer the questions. Use the Internet to check your answers.

1. In 1895, were there … ?
   - aeroplanes
   - cars
   - bicycles
   - electric street lights
   - X-rays
   - Nobel prizes for Science
   - skyscrapers (very tall buildings)
   - telephones
   - players for recorded music
   - cinemas

2. Did people know that … ?
   - the Earth went round the sun
   - atoms were made up of electrons, neutrons and protons
   - there were other galaxies (= systems of stars)

3. What do your answers tell us about H.G. Wells's imagination?

3 Are there things which we do not know now in the 21st century, but which future people may discover? Discuss with other students.

ACTIVITIES

> ... they seemed so weak that I was sure I could fight them.

> We can talk about the **result** of something by using:
> *so* + adjective + (*that*) + result
> *so* + adverb + (*that*) + result
>
> The Traveller's ideas were **so incredible (that)** no one believed them.
> He told his story **so well (that)** everybody listened without speaking.

Grammar: *so* + adjective/adverb + (*that*)

4 PRELIMINARY Complete the second sentence so that it means the same as the first. Use no more than three words.

1. He felt sick because the machine was very fast.
   The machine was .... he felt sick.
2. Because he was very hungry, he ate his dinner first.
   He was .... he ate his dinner first.
3. The people wore few clothes because of the warm weather.
   The weather was .... the people wore few clothes.
4. He wasn't afraid of the little people because of their happy smiles.
   The little people smiled .... he wasn't afraid of them.
5. He liked them because of their sweet way of speaking.
   They spoke .... he liked them.

5 Complete the sentences (1-8) with a suitable ending.

0. The sofa was so comfortable ...
   ... that I didn't want to get up/... that I sat there all day.
1. The weather was so bad ....
2. The beach was so crowded ....
3. They played the music so loudly ....
4. They arrived at the party so late ....
5. The computer game was so good ....
6. That shop is so expensive ....
7. The film is so exciting ....
8. The actor is so talented ....

ACTIVITIES

Listening

6 **PRELIMINARY** Listen to the message. For each question, fill in the missing information in the spaces (1-9).

> **TIME TRAVEL EXHIBITION**
> At the (1) .... Museum
> in (2) .... Street
> Opening time: (3) ....
> Closing time: (4) ....
> Meeting time for Lizzie: (5) ....
> at the (6) .... on the
> (7) .... floor
> Tickets cost (8) £ ....
> Free entry for children (9) ....
> years old

Vocabulary

7 The editor made a joke about time travel: *'Can you tell us the name of the winning horses in the races next week?'* Complete the questions (1-5) about the future with the words in the box. Can you think of other questions about the future?

> exam   job   lottery   numbers   politician
> questions   salary   weather

1 Will the .... be good next Wednesday?
2 Which .... will win the next election?
3 What .... will there be in the History .... ?
4 What .... will I have in 2040? Will I have a high .... ?
5 Can you tell me the winning .... in the .... next Saturday?

ACTIVITIES

Before you read

Ruins

1 When the Time Traveller explores, he sees a lot of ruins. What are the possible reasons for this? Fill each gap (1-4) with one word to complete the idea. If you need help, there are some words at the bottom of the page which you can choose from. Can you add more possible reasons?

1 There has been a ....
2 People are too lazy to .... them.
3 People have moved to .... homes.
4 The climate is .... , so people live outside.

Civilisation

2 **A** What do we mean by the word *civilisation*? The list includes things which are a part of a civilisation. For each idea, give an important example.

> art   buildings   cities   education   government   history
> industry   literature   music   sport   technology

Art - Michelangelo's painting in the Sistine Chapel in Rome

B In the future, civilisation may change. Which are the five most important things for you in the box above? If they disappear in the future, can humans survive (= continue to live)?

C What are the most important things for the Time Traveller in the future world? Choose the five most important things from the box. Explain why they are important.

> finding food and water   learning the language   making friends
> the Time Machine   defending himself   making a map
> keeping healthy   understanding the new civilisation
> pen and paper   a safe place to sleep

Which one is the MOST important for the Time Traveller?

new   repair   war   warmer

CHAPTER **3**

The disappearance

'I left the Time Machine behind me on the small lawn and reached the huge door of the building. More and more little people crowded round me. There were beautiful flowers everywhere.

I passed into a great hall. Everyone was very brightly dressed. I looked strange in my dull clothes with flowers hanging round my neck. They were laughing like excited children and speaking happily. On the numerous tables, there were lots of fruit.

I recognised strawberries and raspberries but most of the fruit were strange types I had never seen before. The little people sat down on cushions on the floor between the tables and immediately began to eat. I discovered later that they only ate fruit. They were all vegetarian. There were no horses, cows, sheep or dogs in this society. Like the dinosaurs, they did not exist.

On this first day, I sat with them and ate the fruit while I looked

CHAPTER 3

around the hall. The building was not in very good condition, with some broken windows and dusty curtains. The nearest marble table was broken. About two hundred people were dining in the hall. Many of them were watching me closely with shining eyes.

I tried to learn their language by showing them things and listening to the names. I even discovered the verb "to eat" in their language. But it wasn't easy to learn as they soon lost interest. I began to disregard the little people. They were friendly, talking and laughing among themselves, but they didn't interact with me. I was alone in a strange future world.

I came out of the great hall and looked around this strange world. Even the flowers were different. The River Thames had changed its position and the beautiful buildings were mostly in ruins.[1] For example, there was a great ruined building made of stone and metal with huge flowering plants growing in the middle of it.

I climbed a hill to obtain a better view. I noticed that there were no small homes anywhere, no typically English houses and cottages. The only buildings were more like palaces.

Society had obviously changed. "Communism," I said to myself. Instead of individual families, people lived in large groups.

I looked back at the people who were following me. They all wore similar clothes and looked similar. Their faces were hairless and their limbs were round and soft. There was no great difference between males and females. Even the children looked like small adults.

I thought carefully about this. Perhaps these changes were the result of a peaceful non-violent society. Families didn't need strong fathers and caring mothers; both sexes shared the work of looking after a limited number of children. It was a continuation

---

1. **in ruins** : broken (for buildings, e.g. the city was in ruins after the bombs).

The disappearance

of the changes that were happening in my own century. This was my idea.

Later I discovered that I was wrong!

I continued climbing. I passed a well,[2] a hole in the ground with a pretty roof. This seemed strange. I arrived at the top of the hill and sat on a seat made of yellow metal. The view was magnificent as the sun set over the valley where the Thames shone like silver. Ruined palaces, silver statues and small domes were scattered across the land. There was no sign of agriculture or of divided fields. The whole Earth had become a garden.

I developed my theory about this world of 802701. The natural sunset in front of me made me think that this time was the sunset of humanity. People did not have urgent needs any more; they had security. Instead of being strong, security had made them weak. In our age, science is improving our health and our agriculture. In the future, science and technology had changed the world completely to suit human beings.

The air was free from insects and the earth was free of weeds;[3] everywhere there were pretty butterflies and lovely flowers and sweet fruits. I saw no evidence of disease. Society was perfect too. The people wore lovely clothes and lived in wonderful buildings. There were no signs of problems or competition. I saw no shops or traffic or advertisements. It was a social paradise.[4]

However, people need danger and difficulty to develop their intelligence and physical strength. People need to be strong, active and efficient in order to survive. While we protect our children with passion and love, in this future world, people did not need these

---

2. **well** : a deep hole in the ground where you can bring up water.
3. **weeds** : useless plants.
4. **paradise** : a perfect place, like heaven.

CHAPTER 3

qualities. They had become passive, unintelligent and satisfied with a life of perfect comfort and security. I saw no signs of war or danger from wild animals. People did not need to work. They had time for pleasure, but as a result, society began to die.

Even art had almost died. These people decorated themselves with flowers and lived in beautiful buildings and enjoyed the sunlight, but they had lost their strength, living without energy or passion. They had few children and their population was decreasing. Yes, it was the sunset of our civilisation.[5] This was my simple explanation. In fact, it was wrong.

As I stood there, thinking about this, the full moon rose and shone with silver light. The bright little people in the distance stopped moving and an owl flew by silently. It was cold on the hill and I decided to descend so that I could find a place to sleep.

I looked for the building which I knew. Then my eye travelled to the White Sphinx, the statue which I had seen when I arrived first of all. There was a silver tree next to it and the flowering bushes. As the moonlight grew stronger, I looked at the little lawn. I looked a second time. "No," I decided, "this must be a different lawn."

But it *was* the lawn. The white face of the Sphinx was turned towards it. Can you imagine my emotions at this moment? The Time Machine had gone!

I felt terrible. I might lose my own time; I might have to live helplessly in this strange new world! The thought of this gripped me by the throat and stopped my breath. Then a huge fear made me run down the slope to the lawn. Although I fell and cut my face, I lost no time but ran on as the warm blood flowed down my cheek.

---

5. **civilisation** : way of life, social development and organisation.

CHAPTER 3

I said to myself, "Perhaps they've moved it, perhaps they've pushed it under the bushes." Nevertheless, I knew really that the machine was lost. I ran as fast as I could. I ran nearly two miles in ten minutes. I am not a young man and my body hurt with the effort. I cursed[6] myself for leaving the machine. I shouted. Nobody answered. I seemed to be alone in the moonlit world.

When I reached the lawn, I saw that my fears were true. There was no trace of the Time Machine. I stood in an empty space. I ran around the lawn angrily, looking in the bushes for the thing. Above me, the huge White Sphinx shone in the moonlight. Its face seemed diseased. It smiled as if it mocked[7] me.

The disappearance of the machine changed all my ideas about this society. I did not believe that the little people had moved the thing. They were too unintelligent and physically weak. Now I had to believe that there was another power in this future world. Something, people or animals, had taken my invention.

I was sure of one thing. Nobody had used my machine to travel in Time. It was impossible. I had removed the levers which controlled it. The machine must be somewhere. But where?

I became mad with fear and anger. A strange white animal ran out of the bushes. I didn't see it clearly in the dim light but I thought it was a deer. I beat the bushes with my hands until my fingers bled. Then, crying loudly, I ran down to the big stone building where the little people were.

---

6. **curse**: wish bad things, say bad words.
7. **mock**: laugh unkindly at someone.

ACTIVITIES

The text and *beyond*

Comprehension check

1 For each question (1-5), choose the correct answer: a, b, c or d.

1 The little people:
   a ☐ ate only strawberries and raspberries.
   b ☐ lived in luxury in a large hall.
   c ☐ enjoyed teaching their language to the Traveller.
   d ☐ were not very interested in the Traveller.

2 Which of these facts about the future world is **not** true?
   a ☐ There were many ruins.
   b ☐ There was a lack of houses and cottages.
   c ☐ Men and women looked similar to one another.
   d ☐ The land was mainly used for farming.

3 What did the Traveller see as the main reason for the changes?
   a ☐ Science had created a perfect, safe world.
   b ☐ Males and females both looked after the children.
   c ☐ The population was decreasing.
   d ☐ There was no more science.

4 He saw that the Time Machine was missing when:
   a ☐ he ran down the hill.
   b ☐ he arrived at the lawn.
   c ☐ the moonlight became brighter.
   d ☐ he saw the Sphinx and the silver tree.

5 The Traveller believed:
   a ☐ the little people had moved the machine.
   b ☐ somebody or something had moved the machine.
   c ☐ the machine had travelled into the past or future.
   d ☐ nobody had moved the machine.

ACTIVITIES

Vocabulary

2 Find the meaning of any of the words in the box which are unfamiliar. Use a dictionary, if necessary. Then complete the gaps (1-12) with the singular or plural forms of some of the words in the box.

Buildings:	house cottage skyscraper palace temple church cabin
Parts:	chimney wall window porch alarm
Materials:	brick concrete steel timber roof tiles ceramic tiles

In the future, people may prefer to live in large groups together, so there might be no individual (**1**) .... To save land, people may have to live in very tall (**2**) .... These are generally built of strong materials, such as (**3**) .... and (**4**) .... If people no longer have kings or queens, there will be no (**5**) .... (**6**) .... and (**7**) .... will still exist if people are religious. Of course, some people may still live in the countryside in small old-fashioned (**8**) .... with roses round the (**9**) .... and the (**10**) .... Or people may live in the forest in (**11**) .... that are built with (**12**) ....
In fact, life may not change much at all. What do you think?

T: GRADE 6

Speaking: learning a foreign language

3 The Time Traveller tries to learn the language of the little people. Answer these questions with your own opinions about learning a language.

1. What do you most enjoy about learning foreign languages?
2. What is most difficult for you? Pronunciation? Grammar? Vocabulary?
3. Which language would you like to learn next?
4. Do you watch films or read books in other languages?
5. What is your advice for someone who wants to learn your language?
6. Why is it good to learn a foreign language?

ACTIVITIES

Interpretation

4 The Time Traveller believed that the changes in society in the year 802701 were already beginning in his own time. Complete the second column with facts about life in 802701. Use words from Chapter 3.

19ᵗʰ/20ᵗʰ/21ˢᵗ century	802701
• More people are vegetarian.	People ate only ....
• Modern medicine	There is no ....
• Modern farming methods	There are no ....
• Modern ideas about relations between men and women	Both sexes shared the work of ....

Speaking: developments in the future

5 In the 21ˢᵗ century, there are many developments that in 1895 seemed impossible. Think of three (e.g. the Internet) and talk about them with another student.

1 Has this invention/development changed the way we live or communicate with others?
2 Has it had any negative effects?
3 Do you think it will continue into the future?
4 What might people in 2100 think of our life now?

Writing

6 **PRELIMINARY** This is part of an email from an English friend. Write a reply asking for more details about the party: date, time, place, other guests. Say if it's a good idea or not. Talk about your own ideas for making a Time Machine. Remember to thank Kevin for the invitation. Write your answer in about 100 words.

It's my birthday next month and I've decided to have a Time Travel Party. My idea is that everyone will come in clothes from the past or from the future. There will be cavemen and women, and cowboys and astronauts, and aliens from the future. Would you like to come? Can you help me make a 'Time Machine'? All the best, Kevin

A short history of science fiction

Science fiction has a very long history. A typical sci-fi story involves a journey to the moon or another planet or star system. In an Indian poem from twenty-five centuries ago, flying machines which can travel into Space are a part of the story. In the second century, a Greek writer, Lucian, described a journey into Space and conversations with aliens[1] from other planets. In his work, there are also giant spiders that live in Space, and a war between the People of the Moon and the People of the Sun. He called his work *A True Story*!

Similarly, time travel is not only a modern idea. In the *Mahabharata*, another ancient Indian story, a king goes to meet a god and discovers that he has also travelled through Time. In an ancient Japanese story, *Urashima Taro*, a fisherman visits a palace under the sea and stays there for three days. When he returns home, he finds that three hundred years have passed. Stories about robots, which are another typical part of modern science fiction, also existed in ancient times. In the *Arabian Nights* from the eighth to the tenth century, there is a story about a mechanical horse that can fly into Space. In one of the stories

---

1. **aliens**: intelligent beings from other planets.

in *The Canterbury Tales* by the English poet Chaucer, there is a metal horse; if you ride the horse and speak into its ear, it will magically take you to any time or place.

These are just a few of the many old stories which are similar to our modern idea of sci-fi. We can also include Thomas More's *Utopia* and Swift's *Gulliver's Travels*, which describe journeys to imaginary [2] countries.

However, as scientific knowledge grew in the nineteenth and twentieth centuries, science fiction also developed. *Frankenstein*, published by the young Mary Shelley in 1818, is one of the most famous sci-fi novels that anyone has ever written. In the book, a young scientist, Victor Frankenstein, tells how he used science to create a person, resulting in terrible events. Films of *Frankenstein* often concentrate on the horror of the story, not the science, but Shelley links the creation of the 'monster' to experiments with electricity and other scientific developments of her time. The use of horror, however, has continued to be a part of popular sci-fi, especially in comics. [3] She also wrote *The Last Man*, about a future in which a plague [4] destroys civilisation; the story ends in the year 2100.

In the second half of the nineteenth century, two authors established science fiction as a major form of literature. One was H.G. Wells himself and the other was Jules Verne, a French author. Verne is famous for novels such as *Journey to the Centre of the Earth*, *From the Earth to the Moon* and *Twenty Thousand Leagues Under the Sea*. He is often called 'the father of science fiction'. He greatly enjoyed reading about science and, as a result, was able to write confidently and knowledgeably about advanced machines in his novels.

---

2. **imaginary** : unreal, created by the imagination.
3. **comics** : magazines which use pictures to tell their stories.
4. **plague** : a terrible illness which spreads quickly and kills people.

Since the time of Verne and Wells, science fiction has continued to progress. It is now found in novels, magazines and films; it has obviously had a great influence on computer games. It is popular not only in Europe and the USA but in Japan, Korea, India and many other nations. Also, many of the ideas in sci-fi have become real, such as robots, space travel and worldwide communication. Twentieth- and twenty-first-century authors such as Isaac Asimov, Ray Bradbury, Brian Aldiss and Ursula K. Le Guin are accepted as important writers. If you're not a fan of science fiction, remember that it covers a very wide field and there is probably a branch of sci-fi which is waiting for you to discover it.

Comprehension check

1 Match (1-8) with (a-g). Choose the most suitable answers. You should use *f* for two of the answers.

Types of story		Examples
1	Time travel	a *The Last Man*
2	Journey into Space	b *Frankenstein*
3	Magic horse	c *Urashima Taro*
4	Science out of control	d Jules Verne's work
5	The end of human life	e *The Canterbury Tales*
6	Stories based on real science	f *A True Story*
7	War in Space	g *Gulliver's Travels*
8	Countries that are imagined	

2 Think about the types of sci-fi in Activity 1. Answer these questions.

1 Which types are most interesting to you? Why?
2 What contact with sci-fi do you have, for example in computer games, in films, on TV, in magazines? Are you a sci-fi fan?
3 Is science fiction an important type of literature?

ACTIVITIES

Before you read

Predicting the story

1 What do you think will happen in Chapter 4? Choose the most likely event from the sentences (1-4).

1 The Time Traveller will find the machine.
2 The little people will attack him and put him in prison.
3 He will fall in love with one of the little people.
4 He will explore the new world but he won't find the machine.

Verbs for *hold* and *pull*

2 Which is the best verb to use in the sentences (1-4)? Use a suitable form of the verb.

to drag = to pull something along the ground, especially if it's heavy
to grab = to take and hold something roughly or angrily
to grasp = to take and hold something, often with enthusiasm or energy
to grip = to hold something firmly, often to keep it under control

1 He .... my hand and welcomed me to his home.
2 She had to .... her suitcase because she couldn't lift it.
3 The Time Traveller .... the lever to keep the speed steady.
4 The thief .... her bag and ran away.

What would you do if ... ?

3 What would you do if ... ?

1 you wanted passionately (= with a lot of feeling and enthusiasm) to travel into the future
2 you travelled into the future but you lost your Time machine
3 you met the people of the future but you didn't understand their language
4 you saw somebody drowning (= to die because of being under the water) in the river

CHAPTER 4

Weena

'The great hall was dark, silent and empty. I slipped on the metal floor and almost broke my leg. I lit a match and went on past the curtains which divided the space.

I came into a second great hall covered with cushions. Many little people were sleeping there. They woke up and stared at me. I was cursing and shouting and the match was something which they had never seen. Matches were a thing of the past, a forgotten invention. "Where is my Time Machine?" I began, shouting like an angry child. I grabbed them with my hands and shook them. Some of them laughed but most were extremely afraid. I wondered if, until that moment, fear was a forgotten emotion for them as they lived in such a secure world. Again, I was wrong.

I threw down the match and ran back through the dining hall into the moonlight. I heard their cries of terror behind me.

Weena

I behaved madly. I had never expected to lose the Time Machine. It was my only way back to my friends, my home and my century. I felt like a strange animal in an unknown world. I ran backwards and forwards, crying out angrily. The night was long and I felt terribly tired but I continued looking everywhere for the machine, in all the most impossible places. I looked for it in the dark moonlit ruins and in the bushes. I touched strange creatures which ran off. At last, I lay on the ground near the Sphinx, crying like a baby before I slept.

When I woke, it was a fresh sunny morning. In the clear light of day, I was able to look at things reasonably. I had been foolish to behave so madly during the night. I argued with myself. "If the machine is lost or destroyed, is it so bad? I must be calm and patient. I must learn more about this future world so that perhaps I can find materials and tools to build another machine. That is my only hope. And this world is so beautiful and interesting that I am lucky to be here."

Probably somebody had taken away the machine and hidden it. I must find the place and recover the machine, by force or by cunning.[1] I stood up and looked around me. I felt so tired and dirty that I wanted to bathe. The morning was fresh and I must be fresh too. I looked calmly around the lawn and when I met some of the little people, I asked them about the machine by using gestures. Some ignored me and others laughed at me, increasing my anger.

Then I found something interesting. I looked down at the grass. There were long marks in the earth. They stretched from the original place of the Time Machine to the bronze pedestal[2] of the White Sphinx. There were also some strange, narrow footprints.

---

1. **cunning** : cleverness, using clever tricks to achieve something.
2. **pedestal** : the part which supports a statue.

CHAPTER 4

There were decorations on the pedestal, with metal panels on the sides. I knocked on these and found that the pedestal was hollow. The panels seemed to be doors that perhaps opened from inside. It was clear that someone or something had dragged the Time Machine and had hidden it inside the Sphinx!

I saw two little people coming to the lawn. I smiled at them and called them to me. I pointed at the bronze pedestal and communicated the idea that I wanted to open the doors. Strangely, they looked at me with horror on their faces. I asked another little person to help me but he reacted in the same way. Angrily, I pulled him to the pedestal but he was so upset that I let him go again.

I knocked hard on the bronze doors. I thought I heard a movement inside the pedestal and a laugh. No, I was mistaken. Then I got a big stone and hammered on the doors with it. I damaged the decoration but I couldn't break through the metal. A crowd of little people heard the noise and came and sat nearby, watching me anxiously. At last, hot and tired, I stopped.

I walked away through the bushes towards the hill. "I must be patient," I told myself. "If I want my machine, I must stop damaging the Sphinx. If the little people want to give me back the Time Machine, I must learn their language and ask for it. If they want to keep it, there is nothing I can do. I must learn more about this world and then perhaps I can solve my problem."

It was comic. I had spent years studying and working in order to create the Time Machine. I wanted passionately [3] to travel into the future. And now I wanted passionately to escape back into my own time. I had made a cunning trap [4] for myself. I laughed aloud.

---

3. **passionately**: with great feeling.
4. **trap**: a place to catch someone or something, e.g. a trap for a tiger.

Weena

I went back to the big palace. The little people soon seemed to forget and were friendly again. When I tried to learn their language, I discovered that it was very simple. There were words which described everyday things and actions, but there were no ways to express ideas. Their sentences usually consisted of only two or three words, so I wasn't able to say or understand anything complicated, like asking about the missing Time Machine.

I climbed different hills to get a view of England in the year 802701. Everywhere was green and rich. I saw more wonderful buildings, more forests, more rivers and hills, more flowers and more gardens. I also found a number of deep circular wells with bronze edges and small roofs like the first one I had seen. When I looked into them, I could see no water. But in all of them, I heard a repeated sound: thud! thud! thud! It was like the beating of a great engine. I also discovered that there was a steady current of air going down into the wells. I threw a piece of paper into one and, instead of slowly floating down, it was pulled rapidly out of sight.

I also saw tall towers here and there. The air above them flickered [5] as if it was hot. I imagined that the wells and the towers were connected. Were they an underground system of ventilation?

It was difficult for me to understand this society. The little people were not interested in explaining anything to me. They seemed to live in a Golden Age of peace and comfort but I didn't understand their customs. For example, I didn't see any places to bury the dead. Also, I didn't see anyone who was sick or old.

Other things were even more difficult to understand. The big palaces were living places, dining halls or sleeping apartments. I found no machinery. These people wore pleasant clothes but how

---

5. **flicker** : move like a flame in the wind.

CHAPTER 4

did they repair or replace them? How did they make their metal shoes? There were no shops or factories or transport. They spent all their time playing or bathing in the river or eating fruit or sleeping. How did their society continue without work?

Why had they taken the Time Machine? Why was the White Sphinx a special place? What were the wells and the towers for?

On the third day, I made a friend. I was watching some of the little people bathing in the river when one of the females got a cramp.[6] She was pulled down by the waters. The river didn't flow strongly but none of the other little people tried to save her. They were too physically weak. She cried out to them but they did nothing. She was drowning[7] before their eyes. Quickly, I took off my coat and jumped into the river. I caught the poor little person and carried her to the land. She was unconscious but I warmed her arms and legs until she woke. Then I left her. I didn't expect her to be grateful. These people seemed to feel no connection with others.

However, I was wrong. This happened in the morning. In the afternoon, I met the little woman again. She cried happily when she saw me and gave me a necklace of flowers which she had made for me herself. I was pleased not to be alone any more. We sat together and tried to have a conversation. There were few words but many smiles. She was like a child. We gave each other more flowers and she kissed my hands. I did the same to hers. I found out that her name was Weena. This was the beginning of a strange friendship. It lasted a week but ended … Well, I will tell you about that later.

---

6. **cramp** : a painful feeling, usually in the legs, especially after too much exercise.
7. **drown** : die because of being under the water.

ACTIVITIES

The text and *beyond*

Comprehension check

1 Complete the sentences (a–h) with a missing word from the story. (Use the first letter to help you.) Then put the sentences in the right order.

- a ☐ I looked into the w……………… and heard a strange sound.
- b ☐ Weena gave me a n……………… of flowers which she'd made.
- c ☐ I k……………… hard on the brass doors of the pedestal.
- d ☐ I p……………… at the doors and asked the little people to help me.
- e ☐ I saw that there were long m……………… in the ground.
- f ☐ I c……………… her out of the water before she d……………… .
- g ☐ I seemed to hear a l……………… inside the pedestal.
- h ☐ I ran backwards and forwards, shouting a……………… .

2 Match these thoughts of the Time Traveller to the items (a–h) above.

- 0 [h] 'I must find the machine or I'll never go back to my time.'
- 1 ☐ 'Maybe I now have a friend.'
- 2 ☐ 'Is there somebody hiding in the Sphinx?'
- 3 ☐ 'If I break into the Sphinx, I'll find the machine.'
- 4 ☐ 'Why didn't her friends help her?'
- 5 ☐ 'How can I make them understand?'

Now imagine the Time Traveller's thoughts for the remaining two situations.

………………………………………………………………………………………
………………………………………………………………………………………
………………………………………………………………………………………
………………………………………………………………………………………

ACTIVITIES

Sentence transformation

3 PRELIMINARY Complete the second sentence so that it means the same as the first. Use no more than three words.

1 My mad behaviour frightened them.
   They ………………………………… my mad behaviour.
2 I let the little person go because he was very upset.
   The little person ………………………………… that I let him go.
3 Learning their language is the way to get their help.
   If I ………………………………… , I can get their help.
4 Somebody locked the machine inside the Sphinx.
   The machine ………………………………… inside the Sphinx.
5 Her friends didn't save Weena.
   Weena ………………………………… her friends.

Vocabulary: feelings

4 In Chapter 4, which characters might have these feelings?

1 fear/fright
2 gratitude
3 surprise
4 confusion
5 anger
6 loneliness

The little people felt fear when the Traveller grabbed them in the dining hall. Weena felt fear when she was drowning in the river.

What are the adjectives which match the feelings (1–6)? For example, if you feel *fear*, you are *afraid* or *frightened*.

5 Choose an adjective or a noun to complete the sentences (1–4).

1 I'm always gr……………………… when somebody gives me something.
2 Some people cannot control their a……………………… .
3 I was very c……………………… by the questions in the exam.
4 If a dog growls at you, you shouldn't show your f……………………… .

When was the last time that you felt these emotions? When did another person feel these emotions about you?

ACTIVITIES

Listening

6 Read the paragraph below. How many of the missing words can you remember or guess? Then listen and check. Write down as many of the missing words as you can. Then check finally by reading the text.

I climbed different hills to get a **(1)** .... of England in the year 802701. Everywhere was green and **(2)** .... I saw more wonderful **(3)** .... , more forests, more rivers and **(4)** .... , more flowers and more **(5)** .... I also found a number of **(6)** .... circular wells with bronze **(7)** .... and small roofs like the first one I had seen. When I looked into them, I could see no **(8)** .... But in all of them, I heard a **(9)** .... sound: thud! thud! thud! It was like the beating of a great **(10)** .... I also discovered that there was a steady **(11)** .... of air going down into the wells. I threw a piece of **(12)** .... into one and, instead of slowly **(13)** .... down, it was pulled **(14)** .... out of **(15)** ....

Adaptation

7 Imagine you are making a film of one or two of the events in Activity 6. Work with another student. Draw some pictures of the scene as it will look on the cinema screen. Include 'speech bubbles' or 'thought bubbles' with words inside them in your drawings. If you are not good at drawing, use 'stick people'. Draw only a face to show a close-up.

Speaking

8 Weena goes swimming in the river and nearly drowns. Discuss these questions with another student.

1 What does this incident show us about ... ?
   a the Time Traveller   **b** the little people

2 *'Everyone should know how to swim.'* Do you agree with this idea? Why?

3 Some people are afraid of the water. What other irrational fears do some people have?

4 What other activities or sports are dangerous?

ACTIVITIES

Before you read

Predicting the story

1 Here are some mysteries from previous chapters:

Chapter 3: 'the beautiful buildings were mostly in ruins.'
'A strange white animal ran out of the bushes.'
Chapter 4: 'someone or something ... had hidden it inside the Sphinx!'
'I heard a repeated sound: thud! thud! thud!'
'I didn't see anyone who was sick or old.'

Before you read Chapter 5, can you think of explanations for these mysteries? By the end of the chapter, you will know the explanations for some of them.

Vocabulary

2 Complete the sentences (1-8) with the words in the box.

> blindly   childlike   faint   ghost   have-nots   industry
> luxury   pleasure-loving   poverty   rudeness   species

1   .... people like to live in ....
2   My uncle enjoys playing silly games; he's very ....
3   The light was very ...,................ so that when I saw a shadow, I thought it was a ....
4   There are many different .... of monkey.
5   The little people have no factories; there is no .... in their world.
6   He was so angry that he drove off .... and crashed the car.
7   People who live in .... with no money are sometimes called the '....................' .
8   Politeness is always better than ....

Which two words from the box would you use to describe the 'little people'?

CHAPTER 5

Two worlds

'ike a child, Weena wanted to be with me always. She followed me everywhere. I decided that this was impossible. I had to find out more about this future world and she only wanted to smile and kiss. I walked so quickly that she was too tired to follow but she cried sadly behind me. She was very fond of me and looked like a little doll. I travelled as far as I could without her but when I came back to the place of the White Sphinx, she was always waiting for me. Although she was a problem, I enjoyed seeing her small figure of white and gold as I came over the hill.

I discovered from her that there was still fear in the world. Although she was brave in the daylight, she hated the dark. She was afraid of shadows and black things. Darkness made her passionate with fear.

I observed how the other little people always slept together in large groups. I never found one outside in the night or sleeping

Two worlds

alone inside. But I was so stupid that I didn't pay attention to this myself. I slept away from the crowds. Weena hated this. But she was so fond of me that most nights she slept by my side with her head on my arm.

Before I met Weena, however, something happened that was difficult to explain. I woke up in the early morning after a strange dream. In the dream, I had been under the sea and sea creatures were feeling my face. As I woke, I saw a grey animal rush out of the room. I tried to go back to sleep but I felt restless and uncomfortable. It was a grey hour of the day when nothing was clear. The darkness was slowly going but everything was colourless and unreal. I got up and went out of the palace to see the sunrise.

The light of the setting moon was mixed with the first light of the sun. The bushes were as black as ink; the sky was sad. And up the hill I thought I could see ghosts![1] I saw white figures. I seemed to see a white monkey-like animal running alone quickly up the hill and a group of these creatures carrying a dark body. They moved in a hurry and soon disappeared among the bushes. I was still half asleep and the light was faint. I did not believe my eyes.

The sky became brighter in the east and the bright colours of the land returned. I looked up and down the hill but I saw no sign of the white creatures. "They were ghosts," I told myself. "I am so many years in the future that there must be billions of ghosts from the past." I laughed at the idea. I remembered the other white creature that I had seen near the Sphinx. But later, when I met Weena, I forgot about these ghostly animals for a time.

It was very hot in the world of 802701. I think that the sun was dying but that one of the planets had fallen into the sun, causing

---

1. **ghosts** : spirits of the dead, returned dead people.

CHAPTER 5

it to explode with energy. One very hot morning, I looked for shelter from the heat in a ruined building. I climbed through the fallen stones into a long narrow room. The windows were blocked. Outside, the light was brilliant but here it was extremely dark. Suddenly, I stopped in surprise. A pair of eyes, reflecting the light outside, was watching me from the blackness!

People have always been afraid of wild animals, wolves or bears or lions. I felt that ancient fear. I remembered the little people's terror in the dark. I stepped forward bravely and spoke. I put out my hand and touched something soft. The eyes moved rapidly and something white ran past me. I turned in fear and saw a strange little figure like a monkey, holding its head down, running across the sunlit space outside. It ran into a block of stone, staggered, and then entered the dark shadows of another ruin.

What was it?

I knew that it was grey-white and had large grey-red eyes. There was some hair on its head and back. But it went too fast for me to see it clearly. Perhaps it had run like an animal or perhaps it ran on two legs, almost touching the ground with its arms.

I followed it into the second ruin. I could not find it at first. But, after a time in the deep darkness, I came to one of those circular wells. I lit a match and, looking down, I could see a small, white, moving creature. It had large bright eyes that looked up at me as it climbed down. It made me shake with sudden fear and disgust. It was like a human spider. I saw that there was a kind of metal ladder attached to the inside walls of the well. Then the match went out, burning my fingers. By the time I had lit another match, the "human spider" had disappeared.

I sat there for a long time looking down that well. Was the thing human? Gradually, I accepted the truth. Human beings had

CHAPTER 5

separated into two species,[2] two distinct animals. One species was the graceful childlike little people of the Upper World. They were pretty, simple and playful. But there was another species: the creatures of the Lower World. These creatures lived by night. They were white ugly creatures, completely different from Weena and her people. But they too were the last examples of the human race.

I thought about the tall towers. I began to suspect the true explanation. What was the role of this white animal in this future society? How was it connected to the lazy pleasure-loving life of the Upper-Worlders? What was hidden at the bottom of the well? I must go down to the underground world to find the answers to my problems. But I was absolutely afraid to go down there even though I told myself that I had no reason for fear.

Two of the beautiful Upper-Worlders came running by. A male was running after a female, throwing flowers at her. They were both laughing happily. However, when they saw me by the well, they became upset. I tried to ask them a question about the well but they immediately turned away. Although I attracted their attention by lighting a match, they refused again to answer me.

But I began to find the answers to my questions as I thought about everything that I had discovered. I linked the wells, the towers and the "ghosts". I realised how the two species were connected in order to create a society that worked.

Here is my idea. Clearly, this second species lived underground. I believed that they rarely came up to the surface as, firstly, they were bleached[3]-white, like white fish that live in the darkness of the deep oceans. Secondly, they had large reflective eyes like cats

---

2. **species** : a type of creature.
3. **bleached** : made pale/colourless either by a chemical or by lack of sunlight.

Two worlds

or owls which catch things by night. Thirdly, they seemed to be uncomfortable in the daylight and to move blindly.

I developed my idea. Beneath my feet, there must be a network of tunnels. This other race of people lived there. I had seen towers and wells all over the land, so they must live in a very large area under the ground. Probably, these Lower-Worlders were the workers. They made the things that the Upper-Worlders needed, their clothes and materials. Yes, that was the answer!

In our own time, there is a gap between "Capitalists" and "Labourers". One class lives in luxury and the other class produces the goods. We tend to use underground space for ugly or noisy things. There is the underground railway of London and other big cities. There are subways, underground workrooms and restaurants. They increase. This is what had happened between our time and 802701. Industry had gradually become an underground thing. There had been deeper and deeper underground factories. Over centuries, the factory workers had spent longer and longer in dark conditions until they had become a different species.

The richer people had continued to live on the surface. They went to university, they enjoyed opera and theatre, they separated themselves from the violence and rudeness of the poor. The gap between them and the workers increased. In our own time, people from a poor family and a rich family may marry. But over time, this had become less common. So, in the end, above the ground there were the "Haves" and below the ground there were the "Have-nots". The Haves enjoyed pleasure and luxury while the Have-nots lived in poor conditions and worked in the factories.

The Have-nots had to live in poverty and pay money to the Haves. They became accustomed to living underground and were probably as happy in their way as the Haves who lived in the Upper

CHAPTER 5

World. The white bloodless appearance of the "human spiders" and the prettiness of the little people were the result.

I had dreamed of a perfect future where people cooperated and lived happily. But in fact, there were two species, one who worked hard underground and one who lived in a lazy paradise. The industrial system had led to this. It was the triumph of the Haves over nature and over other less fortunate men and women. This was my theory at the time.

However, I also saw that the Upper-Worlders had lost their intelligence and strength and energy. This was clear. I discovered later that the two races had different names. The underground workers were the "Morlocks" and the pretty people were the "Eloi".

I still knew very little about the Morlocks. Why had they taken my Time Machine? And if the Eloi were the masters and mistresses, why didn't they give me back my machine? Why were the Eloi afraid of the dark?

ACTIVITIES

The text and *beyond*

Comprehension check

1 Complete the sentences (1-6) about Weena with the required number of words from the chapter.

1 Weena was a problem because she only ……………………… . (5 words)
2 The Traveller enjoyed seeing her when he ……………………… . (4 words)
3 Weena was afraid of ……………………… . (4 words)
4 Weena slept beside me with ……………………… . (5 words)
5 After he woke up, the Traveller saw ……………………… . (3 words)
6 Up the hill, he thought he ……………………… . (3 words)

2 Which phrases refer to the Eloi and which to the Morlocks? Write the numbers in the correct part of the table. Use one of the numbers twice.

0 white like deep-sea fish
00 blind in daylight
1 lazy
2 afraid of darkness
3 monkey-like
4 the 'Have-nots'
5 ugly
6 the 'Haves'
7 graceful
8 weak
9 the workers
10 the last humans
11 living in tunnels
12 no longer intelligent
13 the rich
14 unfriendly

ELOI	MORLOCKS
	0, 00

59

ACTIVITIES

What do you think?

3 The Traveller thinks that the two species were the result of the division between the rich and the workers in the late 19th century. In today's society, how might these things affect the development of the human species in the far future?

- cars (e.g. people lose strength in their legs/they become dependent on cars)
- the Internet
- environmental pollution
- fast food
- robots
- modern medicine
- climate change

Vocabulary: similes

4 Wells writes that the white animal was *like a human spider*. Phrases with *like* are called similes. Can you add more similes to these disgusting and attractive similes?

1 Disgusting/unattractive similes:

like a human spider   *like a human worm*

like a/an ....

2 Attractive similes:

like a beautiful butterfly

like a/an ....

Then complete these sentences.

1 My life is like ....
2 My room is like ....
3 My city/town/village is like ....

ACTIVITIES

Although she was a problem, I enjoyed seeing her small figure …

We use **although** to join two clauses when there is a 'disagreement' between the two ideas.

she was a problem ⇌ *I enjoyed seeing her*

Although can be used at the beginning or in the middle of the sentence:

Although *it rained, we played outside.* = *We played outside* **although** *it rained.*

We can also use **though** (less formal) or **even though** (for emphasis).

Grammar: *although/(even) though/because*

5 Match the two halves of the sentences (0-6) and (a-h). Then join each sentence with *although* or *because*, depending on the connection.

0	h Weena was brave in the daytime.	a	They were afraid of the night.
00	a The Eloi slept inside.	b	She wouldn't answer his questions.
1	☐ The world seemed perfect.	c	They refused to answer him.
2	☐ The Morlocks were white.	d	They were not advanced.
3	☐ Weena wanted to help him.	e	There was still fear.
4	☐ Two different species developed.	f	They lived underground in the dark
5	☐ The Eloi lived in the future.	g	The workers and the rich were divided.
6	☐ He lit a match to attract them.	h	She feared the dark.

0 Although Weena was brave in the daytime, she feared the dark.
00 The Eloi slept inside because they were afraid of the night.

ACTIVITIES

Before you read

Predicting the story

1 What do you think will happen in Chapter 6? Discuss the probability of the events (1-5).

- 0 The Time Traveller will fight the Morlocks.
  The Time Traveller is only one man but there are many Morlocks. It will be difficult for him to fight them without a gun or another modern weapon.
- 1 He will go down one of the wells and return safely.
- 2 The Morlocks will catch the Time Traveller.
- 3 The Eloi will help the Time Traveller to fight the Morlocks.
- 4 Weena will help him to find the Time Machine.
- 5 The Time Traveller will make friends with the Morlocks.

The well

2 **A** What would be the most dangerous and frightening about going down the well?

1 falling
2 meeting the Morlocks
3 entering the darkness
4 not knowing what you will find

B What might the Time Traveller find in the underground world?

1 an underground city
2 machines
3 some of the Eloi in prisons

Asking questions about the story

3 What do you want to know about the Morlocks and the Eloi? Write three more questions. Then read the chapter and see if the answers are there.

1 How dangerous are the Morlocks?
2 Why are the Eloi afraid of the Morlocks?

CHAPTER **6**

Escape from the Morlocks

I asked Weena about the Morlocks and their underground world but she refused to answer. She shook and began to cry the only tears, apart from my own, which I ever saw in that Golden Age. When I saw this, I stopped worrying about the Morlocks. I just wanted to make her happy again. Very soon she began to smile and to clap her hands as I lit a match to please her.

I waited two days before I did anything about my discovery of the world of the Morlocks. I felt disgust when I thought of their pale bodies, the colour of worms or of things that you see in a bottle in a museum. Although they were human, I hated the idea of touching one of them.

I understood why the Eloi did not even want to talk about their underground neighbours.

CHAPTER 6

I did not sleep well the next night because I had so many doubts and strange fears in my mind. I crept[1] into the great hall where the little people were sleeping — Weena was among them that night — and lay down with them. The moon was in its last quarter and the nights were darker. "Perhaps more of the bleached-white Morlocks will come out when the night is completely black," I thought.

I knew what I had to do. I had to go down bravely into the underground world and try to recover the Time Machine. But I could not face the mystery. I needed a friend to come with me into the well. During these days of fear and indecision, I never felt safe. Someone might be creeping up behind me.

I travelled all over the area. In the south-west, towards a great wood, I saw a huge green building. It was larger than the other palaces and ruins and it seemed like an Eastern temple. The pale-green building shone like Chinese porcelain.[2] What was it used for? I decided to go there; however, I realised that first I had to explore the well, to enter the underground world of the Morlocks. I must delay no longer.

In the early morning, I headed for the well in the ruin. Little Weena danced beside me. But when she saw me looking down the well, she became extremely upset. "Goodbye, little Weena," I said, kissing her, and then I leaned into the well, looking for the ladder that went down the inside wall. At first, she watched me in surprise. Then she gave a sad cry and started pulling at me with her little hands. It made me more determined. I shook her off a little roughly and climbed inside the mouth of the well. I saw her terrified face above me and smiled. Then I began to climb down.

---

1. **crept** : move secretly and quietly; from the verb *creep/crept/crept*.
2. **porcelain** : a fine material used for making cups, vases, etc.

Escape from the Morlocks

The well was about two hundred metres deep. The "ladder" consisted of metal bars attached to the wall. I was heavier and taller than a Morlock, so it was more difficult for me to climb down. One of the bars bent under my weight. For a moment, I hung by one hand above the blackness below. My arms and back ached but I had to continue. Looking up, I saw a small circle of blue sky and the black shape of little Weena's head. The thudding sound of a machine blow filled my mind. Everything was completely dark. When I looked up again, Weena had disappeared.

I was terrified of falling and very uncomfortable. "I should go back," I thought, but I continued to descend anyway. At last, I saw a small hole in the wall. I climbed inside and found it was the mouth of a narrow horizontal tunnel. I lay down and rested. My eyes were confused by the unbroken darkness. My body hurt. The air was full of the throb and hum [3] of machinery.

A soft hand touched my face. Immediately, I took my matches and lit one. There were three white creatures, similar to the one that I had seen a few days before in the ruined building. They ran away from the light. Their eyes were unusually large and sensitive. I am sure that they could see me in the darkness and they were not at all afraid of me. But when I made light, they ran into the dark corners of the tunnel. Their eyes stared at me.

I tried to speak to them but it seemed that their language was different from the Upper-World people. Part of me wanted to retreat but instead I decided to head towards the sound of the machinery. Soon, I came to a large open area. I lit another match and saw that I had reached a huge cave. It stretched into the darkness beyond the light of my match.

---

3. **throb and hum** : a repeated beating movement and a low continuous sound.

CHAPTER 6

There were the great shapes of machines. The Morlocks sheltered in the black shadows from the light of the match. The air was not clean and I could smell fresh blood. Some way away, there was a white metal table with food on it. Unlike the Eloi who lived only on fruit, the Morlocks ate meat. I wondered what animal they had killed. The piece of meat on the table was large and red. Nothing was clear. The smell, the black shapes and shadows, the horrific figures of the Morlocks waiting to attack me after the light ended. And then the match *did* burn out. It burnt my fingers and dropped to the floor, a small red spot.

I had not prepared for an experience like this. When I had first had the idea of time travel, I had imagined a future world which would be far more modern than my own. I had travelled into the future without guns or medicine or even a camera! I stood in the darkness with only my natural weapons[4] — hands, feet and teeth.

Worse than this, I had few matches. I had brought a box of matches with me, but only four remained. I hadn't known that my matches were my main weapon against the Morlocks. As I stood in the dark, a hand touched mine. Fingers felt all over my face. The Morlocks had an unpleasant smell. I heard their breathing. A hand tried to take the box of matches and other hands pulled at my clothes. The unseen creatures examined me — it was horrible.

I knew nothing about them. How did they think? What were their lives like? What emotions did they have? I shouted at them as loudly as I could. They moved back but then came close again. They touched me more boldly and spoke softly to one another, making strange noises. I shivered and shouted again. This time, they were not so afraid and they seemed to laugh strangely.

---

4. **weapons** : things useful for defending or attacking, such as guns and knives.

CHAPTER 6

I lit another match and burnt a piece of paper to increase the light. I ran back to the narrow tunnel. But the rushing air stopped burning my match. In the blackness, I heard the Morlocks coming after me with a sound like the wind in the leaves or the falling rain.

In a moment, several hands clutched[5] me. They were trying to drag me back. I lit another match and held it in their faces. You cannot imagine how horribly inhuman they were. I saw their pale chinless faces and great lidless pinkish-grey eyes. But I didn't stay to look! I retreated again and, when my second match had ended, I lit a third. It had almost burned out when I reached the well-shaft. I lay down and reached for the ladder of metal bars. As I did so, hands grasped my legs from behind. I was pulled backwards.

I lit my last match. Almost immediately, it went out. But I had my hands on the bars now and I kicked out violently. I escaped from the hands of the Morlocks and climbed quickly upwards while they looked after me. One little Morlock followed me for some way and almost pulled off my boot. But at last I was free from them all.

The climb was long and hard. I began to feel sick and I almost fell down. At last, however, I reached the mouth of the well and climbed out. I staggered out of the ruin into the sunlight. It blinded me. I fell on my face. Even the earth smelt fresh and clean. Then I remember Weena kissing my hands and ears and the voices of the other Eloi. After that, for a time, I was unconscious.

When I woke, I realised that this future world was more dangerous than I had ever imagined.

---

5. **clutch** : hold tightly.

ACTIVITIES

The text and *beyond*

Comprehension check

1 For each question (1-5), choose the correct answer: a, b, c or d.

1 The Traveller disliked the Morlocks because:
   a ☐ of their appearance.
   b ☐ they lived underground.
   c ☐ they were not human.
   d ☐ Weena was terrified of them.

2 When he climbed down the well:
   a ☐ he moved rapidly.
   b ☐ he could see Weena's head all the time.
   c ☐ he nearly fell.
   d ☐ everything was dark and silent.

3 The Morlocks ran away because:
   a ☐ they were afraid of the Traveller.
   b ☐ they had never seen matches before.
   c ☐ they had very sensitive eyes.
   d ☐ they were afraid of the heat.

4 The Traveller:
   a ☐ was well-prepared for this adventure.
   b ☐ lost the matches.
   c ☐ could smell, feel and hear the Morlocks.
   d ☐ couldn't see the Morlocks while he was underground.

5 During this adventure, the Traveller:
   a ☐ lost a boot.
   b ☐ used all his matches.
   c ☐ had to kill one of the Morlocks.
   d ☐ used all his matches except one.

ACTIVITIES

Speaking and writing

2 With another student, take turns to state facts about the world in 802701.

A: There are two types of human, the Eloi and the Morlocks.
B: The Eloi are small and graceful.
C: The Morlocks …

Continue until you can think of no more facts. Use your ideas to write a description of the future world of the novel in 70 to 100 words. Include the most important facts.

Interpretation

3 How far do you agree or disagree with these opinions? Give reasons. Give each opinion a score:

5 = strongly agree   **4** = agree   **3** = perhaps agree
2 = disagree   **1** = strongly disagree

1 The Traveller is very brave.
2 He achieved nothing by going down the well.
3 Weena is a problem for him.
4 I feel sorry for the Morlocks.
5 Chapter 6 is very exciting.

Vocabulary: movement

4 The Traveller is afraid that the Morlocks might 'creep' up behind him. To creep is 'to move silently and secretly'. Complete the sentences (1–8) with the words in the box. All the words describe ways of moving.

> crawl   dash   limp   prowl   slip   stride   stroll   wander

1 You may ………………………… on an icy street.
2 People ………………………… to catch a train if they're late.
3 Thieves ………………………… , looking for a house to rob.
4 Babies ………………………… before they can walk.

ACTIVITIES

5 If you hurt an ankle, you may ……………………………… .
6 'To walk with long powerful steps' is 'to ……………………………… '.
7 People may ……………………………… in the park to relax.
8 I don't like to follow a fixed path, I like to ……………………………… .

Matching

5 **PRELIMINARY** The people below all enjoy adventure. Decide which activity (a-f) would be most suitable for each person (1-4).

1 ☐ Joss loves water sports from jet-skiing to wind-surfing. But he always wears a life-jacket because he isn't a strong swimmer. He loves to be outdoors in nature and to breathe the cool, fresh air.

2 ☐ Cathy grew up in Nigeria and doesn't mind the heat. She loves to get completely away from people and to experience wild places. She suffers from a fear of heights.

3 ☐ Lorna suffers from claustrophobia, a fear of small spaces. But otherwise she loves exploring new environments with others and to watch wildlife.

4 ☐ Harry always loves to do something new and dangerous. He's swum across lakes, climbed mountains, flown over volcanoes and spent days camping in extreme environments. Where can he go next?

a **Hill-climbing** Get up and away from the pollution and stress of everyday city life by joining our climbing groups.

b **Desert-trekking** Walk in some of the world's hottest and loneliest places.

c **Parachuting** Are you brave enough to step out of a plane and see the world from above? Be alone in the silence of the skies.

d **Long-distance swimming** Crossing from England to France is just one of the challenges for long-distance swimmers to enjoy.

e **Pot-holing** You can join adventurous pot-holers and explore the dark world of underground caves and tunnels.

f **Rain-forest camping** Join groups of campers and make contact with tropical rainforest animals and birds.

ACTIVITIES

Before you read

Predicting the story

1 The next chapter is *The journey to the Porcelain Palace.* Answer these questions.

1. Why might the Traveller want to go to the Porcelain Palace?
2. How can he protect himself against the Morlocks during the journey?
3. Is it a good or a bad idea to take Weena with him?
4. What kind of place is most dangerous for the Traveller during the journey?
5. The Eloi eat fruit. What might the Morlocks eat?
6. Why is Weena afraid of the 'Dark Night' and what is it, do you think?

2 The Porcelain Palace used to look like this. What was it? Which things in the pictures can you name?

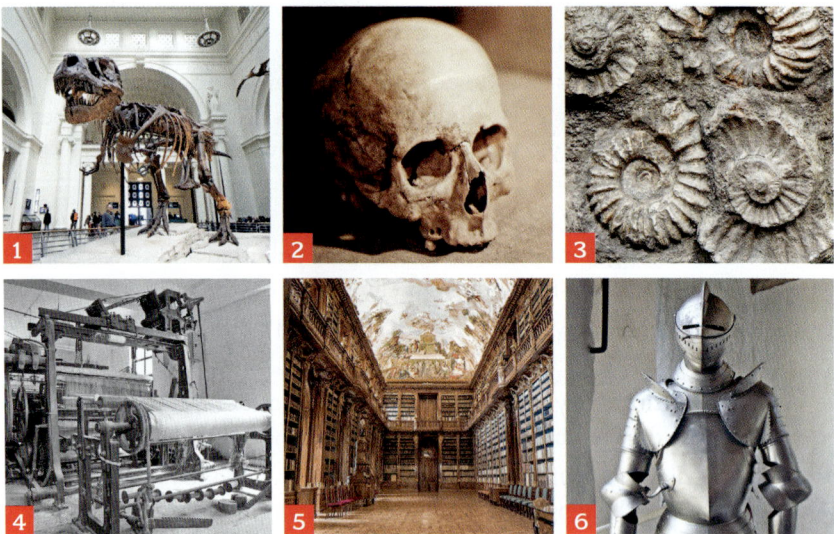

Are there any things in an old museum that might be useful for the Time Traveller?

CHAPTER 7

The journey to the Porcelain Palace

'My situation seemed worse than before. I had hoped previously that I would escape from the future and return to the present. If I waited long enough, the little people would return the Time Machine. But now I knew that the cruel and dangerous Morlocks had stolen the machine, not the Eloi. I had a powerful enemy.

Weena had often spoken to me about the "Dark Night". I didn't understand her fear before but now I did. Each night, the darkness was longer as the moon grew smaller. I shared the fear of the Upper-World people. What horrible things did the Morlocks do during the nights of the new moon?

I had changed my ideas about the relationship between the two species of human beings. Long ago, the Eloi had been the top people

CHAPTER 7

who had controlled their workers, the Morlocks. The Eloi had been the rich powerful people and the Morlocks had been the powerless ones. But this had all changed. The Eloi were like the kings of history who lost their strength. They were beautiful and playful, but weak. They still owned the Upper World but only because the Morlocks could not live in the daylight. And the Morlocks still made their clothes and other necessary things. But the power had moved from the Eloi to the Morlocks, from the Haves to the Have-nots. The end of the beautiful, easy life of the Eloi would come soon. Many thousands of years ago, human beings had forced their brother human beings out of the luxury and the sunshine. And now that brother was coming back — changed!

Already, fear had returned to the lives of the Eloi. Suddenly, I remembered the meat which I had seen in the Under World. The image floated into my mind by chance: the red meat on the metal table. Where did the meat come from?

But I came from a modern age when fear and mystery had been overcome. I could defend myself. I decided to make weapons and to find a safe place where I would sleep. I realised that until now the Morlocks had watched me at night and examined me.

During the afternoon, I walked along the valley of the Thames, looking for a place that I could defend. I found nothing suitable. I knew that the Morlocks could climb quickly and skilfully, so all the trees and ruined buildings were not safe against them. Then I remembered the Green Porcelain Palace that I had seen in the distance. That was the answer.

In the evening, with Weena riding on my back, I headed up the hills towards the south-west. The palace was further than I thought. In addition, my shoes were falling to pieces so that it was difficult to walk quickly. They were old shoes that I used to wear at

CHAPTER 7

home. It was long past sunset when I at last saw the palace, a black shape against the yellowish sky.

Weena had been very happy when I carried her on my back but soon she preferred to run beside me. She picked flowers and placed them in my pockets. The Eloi did not have pockets in their clothes, so they were strange and new to Weena. And look! This is what I found in the pockets of my jacket after I came back to the present.'

The Time Traveller paused, put his hand in his pocket and silently placed two dead flowers, large and white, on the table. Then he continued telling us his story.

'Weena grew tired and wanted to go back. I pointed at the distant towers of the Palace of Green Porcelain and explained with gestures that we would be safe there. As the quiet evening progressed, the world seemed to pause. The wind stopped in the trees. The sky was clear, distant and empty. My fear returned, I listened to every sudden sound. I knew that beneath my feet, underground, the Morlocks were moving, waiting for the dark. I had invaded their tunnels and they saw that as a sign of war.

We walked on in the increasing darkness. The blue of the sky became darker and the stars came out. I could almost not see the ground and the trees grew black. Weena's fears and tiredness increased. As the darkness grew deeper, she put her arms round my neck and, closing her eyes, tightly pressed her face against my shoulder. Like this, we went down into a valley, crossed a little river and passed by some buildings. There was a statue and some beautiful flowering bushes. I had seen no sign of the Morlocks. But it was still early.

As we climbed the next hill, I saw a thick dark wood in front of us. It seemed endless and stretched from right to left. I was very

The journey to the Porcelain Palace

tired with sore[1] feet, so I lowered Weena from my shoulders and sat down on the grass. I couldn't see the Porcelain Palace any more. Which was the right direction? What was inside the darkness of the wood? How could I find my way through the thick trees?

I decided to pass the night on the open hill. Luckily, Weena was fast asleep. I wrapped her in my jacket and sat beside her, waiting for the moon. The hill was quiet but from time to time the noise of living things came from the wood. The stars shone clearly above me. They were in different places from the stars in our time. But the Milky Way seemed to me to be the same stream of stars as I knew. There was a red star which was new to me. And one bright planet shone kindly and steadily like the face of an old friend.

As I looked at these stars, I thought of the huge distances of the Universe and of Time. My own troubles seemed small. In the centuries I had travelled through, all the human traditions, literature, organisations, nations, languages, hopes, memories had disappeared. Instead, there were these weak creatures, the Eloi, who had forgotten everything, and the bleached-white underground beings who were more like animals than people. Then I thought of the "Great Fear" between the two species. For the first time, I saw clearly where the meat on the table of the Morlocks had come from. It was too horrible! I looked at little Weena sleeping beside me, her face white and like a star.

Through the long night, I tried to forget the Morlocks and studied the stars. I slept a little at times. Then the old moon rose, thin and pale. At last morning came. I had seen no Morlocks on the hill during the night. I stood up and found that my foot hurt terribly, so I threw my broken shoes away.

---

1. **sore**: painful.

CHAPTER 7

I woke Weena and we went down into the wood, which was green and pleasant. We found some fruit to eat. We soon met other little people, laughing and dancing in the sunlight. I thought again of the meat I had seen among the Morlocks. I was sure now. I felt deeply sorry for these last weak people, the Eloi. I understood that at some time in the history of the human race, the Morlocks had not had enough food. Perhaps they began to eat rats and other animals. Even in our own time, people eat many different types of food. It was easy for the Morlocks to little by little decide that they would eat the flesh[2] of others. After all, the gap between the Morlocks and the Eloi was so great that they seemed like a separate species. The Morlocks were no longer intelligent enough to feel guilty. To them, the Eloi were like cows or sheep. The Morlocks kept them alive as a supply of food. I looked at Weena dancing at my side.

This was the dark secret of this future world.

Time had punished the rich. They had lived from the work of others and now they were the victims. It was impossible to feel angry with the Eloi. Even though they had lost their intelligence and their traditions, they had remained recognisably human. I felt sympathy for them and a horror of the Morlocks.

I was unsure about my next actions. I had to find a safe place and to make weapons. I also hoped to find a method of making fire. Nothing was a more efficient weapon against the Morlocks than light. Then I wanted to make something that could break open the bronze doors of the White Sphinx. I could escape in the Time Machine and bring Weena with me. With these ideas in my mind, I headed on towards the palace.

---

2. **flesh** : the 'meat' of our bodies; our skin covers our flesh.

The journey to the Porcelain Palace

When we arrived at the Palace of Green Porcelain it was empty and ruined. There was broken glass in the windows and green metal had fallen from its walls. It stood on a hill and I could see the sea in the distance. It covered part of our present city of London.

The palace was really made of porcelain and there was strange writing on the front. Weena, like all the Eloi, had forgotten about a written language and could not read it. She always seemed to me more human than she was, perhaps because she was able to love.

We found a long room inside, like a museum. Dust covered everything. There was a huge object in the middle of the hall; I recognised it as the skeleton of a dinosaur, perhaps a Megalitherium. The skull and some bones lay on the floor. Yes, the place really was a museum, like the Natural History Museum in London. I found glass cases with fossils[3] inside on the shelves. The whole place was silent. Weena stopped playing with one of the things and came and stood beside me and held my hand.

I was amazed by the size of the place. There might even be a library here. I found different departments with various things in them. There was a great hall with old machines.

Suddenly, Weena came very close. She had noticed that the room became very dark at one end. The windows were blocked by earth. I looked down at the dust on the floor and saw a number of small footprints. The Morlocks had been here.

Then, from the darkness at the end of the hall, the sounds of movement came.

---

3. **fossils** : the remains in rock of dead creatures from the past.

ACTIVITIES

The text and *beyond*

Comprehension check

1 For each sentence answer (T) True or (F) False.

		T	F
1	The Eloi are afraid of the time of the full moon.	☐	☐
2	The Morlocks had stopped making things for the Eloi.	☐	☐
3	It was only safe to sleep in a tree or a ruined building.	☐	☐
4	The Traveller kept the flowers that Weena had given him.	☐	☐
5	When he looked at the stars, he felt calmer.	☐	☐
6	The Morlocks kept cows and sheep to eat.	☐	☐
7	The Eloi are no longer as intelligent as the people who built the museum.	☐	☐
8	The Traveller saw Morlocks in the Porcelain Palace.	☐	☐

Interpretation

2 The Time Traveller has formed different ideas about the situation in 802701. Look at the sentences (1-6) and write the chapter number in which the idea **first** occurs.

IDEA	CHAPTER
0 People had become passive and unintelligent because they had security.	3
1 The Morlocks realised that the Eloi were a supply of food for them.	☐
2 The towers and wells were part of a mystery. How did the people survive?	☐
3 The Eloi and Morlocks come from the rich and the workers.	☐
4 The people of the future are not intelligent or advanced.	☐
5 People had decided to live in groups; male and female roles had changed.	☐
6 The Morlocks were dangerous; they had machines and ate meat.	☐

ACTIVITIES

It was too horrible to imagine!

We can use **too** + **adjective** + **to** + **verb** in this way:
*Weena was **too weak to continue**.* = She could not continue because she was very weak.
We can express the same idea using:
so + **adjective** + **that** + (**not**) + **verb**
*She was **so weak that** she **couldn't continue**.*
(**not**) + **adjective** + **enough** + **to** + **verb**
*She **wasn't strong enough to continue**.*
(**not**) + **verb** + **enough** + **noun** + **to** + **verb**
*She **didn't have enough strength to continue**.*

Grammar: *too/so/enough*

3 PRELIMINARY Complete the second sentence so that it means the same as the first. Use no more than three words.

1. His story was too strange to believe.
   His story was ……………………………… we couldn't believe it.
2. The Morlocks were so afraid that they couldn't approach the fire.
   The Morlocks were ……………………………… approach the fire.
3. The other Eloi were too cowardly[1] to fight the Morlocks.
   The other Eloi weren't ……………………………… fight the Morlocks.
4. The palace wasn't close enough to reach in one day.
   The palace was ……………………………… that they couldn't reach it in one day.
5. It was so dark that they couldn't see anything.
   There wasn't ……………………………… see anything.

Writing

4 Write a story or a diary entry about one of these situations.

- being locked in a museum with the Egyptian mummies
- breaking a very valuable ancient vase in a museum
- a robbery at an art gallery
- a museum where the things come alive after dark

---

1. **cowardly**: afraid.

ACTIVITIES

T: GRADE 6

Speaking: rules and regulations

5 To protect themselves, the Eloi have certain rules:
Do not go out in the dark. Do not sleep alone. Keep away from the wells.
Work with another student, asking and answering these questions about rules and regulations.

1 Are there too many rules and regulations in your life? Which rules would you change?
2 What rules and regulations should parents have for children under 12 about … ?
   a using the Internet
   b bedtime
   c going out alone
   d doing schoolwork
3 What rules and regulations should parents have for teenagers about a, b, c and d above?
4 What are rules for? To keep us safe or to control us?
5 What rules should there be for advertisers?
6 Do rules keep us safe? Or do they create a prison?

Internet project: museums

6 Use the Internet to find information about museums and art galleries in the United Kingdom.
Here are some things that I discovered about the British Museum in London.

> Opening times: daily 10.00–17.30
> Open late on Fridays until 20.30
> Entry: free for adults and families
> Location: Great Russell Street, London WC1B 3DG
> Exhibits include: Egyptian mummies; other exhibits from all over the world

1 Find similar information about another museum or gallery in:
   a London
   b another city in the UK
   c New York
   d your country
2 Search for 'unusual museums' using a search engine like Google. Report back to other students. Who found the most unusual museum?

Is time travel possible?

On June 9th, 2009, Stephen Hawking, the famous scientist and author of the best-selling book *A Brief History of Time*, held a party with champagne and lots of food. **After** the party, he sent out invitations to Time Travellers; he gave the date and location of the party. If any future Time Travellers saw the invitations on the Internet or in some other way, they would travel back in Time to attend the party. However, nobody came. Perhaps nobody in the future was able to use a Time Machine to come back to the year 2009. Does this prove that time travel will never exist?

H.G. Wells has had a big influence on authors and film-makers, who have often invented new stories about human beings travelling in Time. In our imagination, we can go back to the time of the first humans or go forward to the year 802701. However, scientists have various ideas about the possibility of time travel in the real world.

There are several films, such as *Stargate* (1994), which have used the idea of a 'wormhole' as the 'door' to another time or universe. Wormholes are holes in Time. Many scientists think that the ideas of Einstein suggest that wormholes really exist. Even if they do exist, wormholes would be so small that it would certainly be impossible for a person to travel through them to another time.

However, Stephen Hawking believes that time travel is possible if scientists can discover a method of catching wormholes and making them bigger. Our modern technology is not able to do this and perhaps people will never be able to use wormholes in this way because it would need a huge amount of energy. Some scientists have made plans of how to build a Time Machine. But they also say that some of the necessary materials do not exist in our universe!

Philosophers doubt if it is possible to travel into the past. If we went into the past, we would be able to change the present. For example, we could go back and stop a war or kill a leader of a country. Then history would change. This seems a crazy situation. Also, nobody has ever met a Time Traveller from the future. If people are able to travel in Time, why don't they come back to give us advice? Sometimes people think that we can prove that time travel happens. For example, they say that a man is wearing modern sunglasses in a photo from 1941 or a woman is using a mobile phone in a 1928 film. However, when we look at this closely, we can easily explain why the image is fake or we have interpreted it wrongly.[1]

However, there are some scientists, including Stephen Hawking, who believe that travel into the future may happen one day. They say that Time runs at different speeds in different situations. Satellites[2] in Space are an example of this. Time runs slower in Space, so it is necessary to change the time on the clocks in the satellites to keep them the same as clocks on Earth. The difference is tiny, less than one billionth of a second each day, but it proves that Einstein was right when he suggested that Time does not always run at the same speed.

1. **interpret it wrongly** : explain the meaning of it wrongly; see it in the wrong way.
2. **satellites** : man-made objects in Space which, for example, help with sending television signals.

Hawking suggests that if we can invent a machine which travels at nearly the speed of light, we can travel into the future. It is difficult for us to imagine this, but two hundred years ago, few believed that moving pictures, telephones or flying machines were possible.

As you can see, the possibility of time travel depends on lots of unanswered questions. For example:

- Do wormholes exist?
- Will time travel technology improve?
- How fast can we travel?
- Have people already travelled into the past?
- Why did nobody come to the Time Travellers' party?

Perhaps Time is like a river and one day we can learn how to swim in it. If you are interested in these complicated ideas, use the Internet or an encyclopaedia to find out more.

Comprehension check

1 For each sentence answer (T) True or (F) False. Show your answers to another student and check whether she/he agrees. Discuss any differences in your answers.

T F

1. We know that nobody in the future saw the invitations.
2. Stephen Hawking has invented a Time Machine.
3. Wormholes may exist.
4. We will probably be able to use wormholes for time travel in the future.
5. Time travel into the past is a crazy idea.
6. Time travel into the future is also a crazy idea.
7. Many people in the past did not imagine that our modern technology was possible.
8. The five questions at the end of the dossier are difficult to answer.
9. The information in the dossier suggests that travel into the future is more likely than travel into the past.

ACTIVITIES

Before you read

Location

1 The Time Traveller is in different locations during the story. Put the letters in order to find the locations (1-8). Then answer the questions.

1 the krad dowo ....
2 the Procineal lacaPe ....
3 the nawl ....
4 the Shipnx ....
5 the ewll ....
6 the reriv ....
7 the aGret aHll ....
8 the dunredrogun ....

1 Which of these places is farthest from the Time Machine?
2 What must the Traveller and Weena pass through on their way back?
3 Where do the little people eat and sleep?
4 Where is the Time Machine?
5 At night, which place do the Morlocks leave?

Vocabulary

2 You will meet many words related to fighting and fire during Chapter 8. Match the words (1-9) with the definitions (a-i).

1 ☐ ammunition
2 ☐ armour
3 ☐ burn
4 ☐ camphor
5 ☐ explosives
6 ☐ dynamite
7 ☐ flame
8 ☐ punch
9 ☐ spark

a to be on fire; to hurt someone with fire or anything hot
b strong metal clothes which people used to wear in wars
c the red or yellow part of a fire which you can see
d mixtures of chemicals which can explode
e to hit hard with your closed hand
f a chemical material that burns easily with a strong light
g things that are used in weapons, for example bullets for guns
h this explodes with great power; it is a type of '5'
i a very small and bright 'piece of fire'; smaller than '7'

CHAPTER **8**

Fire!

"I needed a weapon. One of the machines in the museum had a lever coming from it. I climbed up and grasped this lever in my hands, pulling on it until it broke. It was strong and heavy. I returned to Weena with this weapon in my hand, ready to break the head of any Morlock who attacked us. I wanted to kill a Morlock; perhaps it was inhuman to want to kill one of my own descendants[1] but it was impossible to think of them as human.

With the weapon in one hand and Weena's hand in the other, I went into another large hall. Rags,[2] like tattered[3] flags, hung from both sides. They were the remains of books that had fallen

---

1. **descendants** : anyone who comes after you in your family; your children, your children's children, etc.
2. **rags** : old pieces of cloth.
3. **tattered** : broken.

CHAPTER 8

to pieces. The printed writing had all disappeared; only the covers and tattered paper remained. I thought of all the work and wasted hours of the writers. Perhaps even one of my own books on physics was there.

We went up some stairs in the ruined museum and found a department of chemistry. I hoped to find something useful here. I examined all the cases and found a box of matches. I tried one. Even after hundreds, perhaps thousands of years, it produced a flame! This was my most powerful weapon against the Morlocks.

"Dance!" I said to Weena in her language.

There, in the ruined museum, on the carpets of dust, I celebrated with a strange mad dance of happiness and an old song.

In another glass case, I found a chemical substance. It was camphor. I remembered that it burnt easily with a bright flame. I put it in my pocket. I found nothing else useful, no explosives, but I felt very happy with my discoveries.

I spent a long afternoon with Weena in this fascinating ruin. There was a hall of armour with old weapons but I decided my heavy lever was more useful, either for killing Morlocks or for breaking through the bronze doors of the White Sphinx. There were guns but no ammunition. In another place, there were statues of gods from all over the world. I wrote my name with my finger in the dust on the nose of one of them!

In another place, I found some dynamite. But it wasn't real. It was only for display.

We found some fruit trees in a courtyard, so we ate and rested. Then we set out in the direction of the dark forest. We would build a fire and sleep in the countryside. In the morning, I would get the Time Machine. I would travel back to my own time with Weena.

Fire!

I collected sticks and grass for the fire and carried them with us. This made us slow and as we reached the wood, the daylight was ending. Weena was afraid of entering the wood but I was determined to pass through to the other side before we slept.

There was a noise in the bushes. I saw three figures — Morlocks! I did not feel safe. "We'll go through the forest and find a better resting place," I thought. "The matches and camphor will help to defend us against the enemy. Weena is afraid of the dark wood." But if we stayed here, the Morlocks would kill us.

I had a sudden idea. I decided to make a fire and leave it behind us as a way to stop the Morlocks from following. I lit the firewood we had collected. Fire was a new thing in this future world where so much human knowledge had disappeared.

Weena had never seen flames. She wanted to run into it and play with it. I stopped her and carried her with me into the black wood. For a little way, the fire lit our path. I looked back and saw that the flames had spread into the bushes. A curved line of fire ran over the hill. I laughed at that and went forward. Weena clung to me. It was difficult to see. I wasn't able to light a match because with one hand I supported Weena and in the other I held my weapon, my iron bar.

I heard nothing except the twigs[4] breaking under my feet, the wind in the trees above and my own breathing. Then I heard another sound. It was the footsteps of Morlocks and the same strange noises I had heard in the Under-World. There were clearly several Morlocks and they were getting nearer. A minute later, I felt fingers pulling at my coat, then at my arm. Weena shook violently and became completely still.

---

4. **twigs**: small pieces of wood from the branches.

CHAPTER 8

It was time to light a match. But to get one, I had to put Weena down. I did so and searched in my pockets. A fight began in the darkness round my knees as the Morlocks tried to take Weena. Soft little hands crept over my coat and back and touched my neck. Then the match burst into flame. I saw the white backs of the Morlocks running away. I quickly took a piece of camphor and prepared to light it. Then I looked at Weena. She was lying at my feet, not moving, with her face to the ground. Suddenly afraid, I bent down. She was hardly breathing. I lit the camphor and drove the Morlocks into the shadows. I knelt down and lifted her. The wood behind us seemed full of the movement of a great crowd.

Weena had fainted. I put her carefully on my shoulder and started to move on. But which was the right direction? Was I facing in the direction of the Green Palace or the Sphinx? I decided to camp there until daylight. I collected sticks and leaves. The eyes of the Morlocks glowed in the light of the burning camphor.

When it stopped burning, I lit a match. Two white figures ran away from the unconscious body of Weena. One was blinded by the light and came straight towards me. I hit him hard and he staggered away and fell down. I lit more camphor and continued collecting material for a fire. Using dry branches, I soon had a smoky fire. I turned to Weena and tried to revive her but she was like a dead person. Was she breathing? I couldn't tell.

The smoke of the fire and the smell of the camphor made me sleepy. The fire would burn for an hour. I sat down. It seemed as if my head dropped for only a minute and then I woke. Everything was dark and the Morlocks had their hands on me. I freed myself and felt in my pockets. But the matches had gone!

Then they held me again. I knew what had happened. I had slept and the fire had gone out. It was the end. It was death.

CHAPTER **8**

The forest seemed full of the smell of burning wood. The Morlocks caught me by the neck, the hair and the arms, pulling me down. It was an indescribable horror to have all these soft creatures on top of me. I was trapped. I felt little teeth at my neck. I rolled over and my hand fell on the iron bar. I rose to my feet, shaking off the human rats, and swung the weapon at the level of their faces. Bone cracked.[5] For a moment I was free.

I felt the extreme happiness that often comes with fighting. I knew that both Weena and I were lost but I was determined to make the Morlocks pay for their meat. I stood with my back to a tree and swung the iron bar. The wood was full of their movement and their cries. A minute passed. Their voices rose and became more excited but none of them came near me. I stared into the blackness. Were the Morlocks afraid?

The darkness began to glow. I was able to see the Morlocks on the ground near me and then I saw others, running through the wood away from me. Their backs were no longer white, but reddish. The air above me was full of red sparks. I understood the smell of burning, the growing sound of a fire, the Morlocks' escape.

Stepping forward from the tree, I could see the burning forest. It was the first fire I had lit, eating up the trees. I looked for Weena but she was gone. The fire hissed and crackled[6] as each new tree burst into flame. I followed the Morlocks out of the forest but the fire blocked me and I had to turn. At last I came into an open space. A blinded Morlock ran past me straight into the fire itself.

I saw the most horrible scene of all. The burning arms of the wood enclosed the space with yellow flames. On a small hill in

---

5. **crack** : break with a sharp sound.
6. **hiss and crackle** : these words describe the sounds of the fire.

Fire!

the middle, thirty or forty Morlocks staggered into one another, blinded by the light. At first, I struck them with my weapon, killing one and injuring more. But when I saw them groping[7] and moaning, I was sure that they were absolutely helpless. I hit them no more.

Sometimes one came towards me and I quickly avoided him with a shock of horror. The fire flamed brightly so that I could walk among them, looking for Weena. There was no sign of her. At last I sat down and watched this strange crowd of blind things as they moved around madly in the light and heat of the fire. The smoke spread rapidly across the sky and, like things of another world, the little stars shone. Two or three Morlocks crashed into me and I drove them away with my hands.

The nightmare lasted for the rest of the night. I hit the ground in anger, I got up and sat down again, I walked from here to there. I rubbed my eyes and called to God. Three times I saw Morlocks put their heads down and rush into the flames. But at last, as the red of the fire died, above the black smoke and the burnt trees, the white light of day arrived.

I searched again for Weena without finding her. It was clear that they had left her in the forest in the middle of the fire. At least, they had not taken her for their meat. The horrible death of little Weena left me terribly alone. It was time to head for the hiding place of the Time Machine and to return to my own century.

---

7. **grope** : try to find their way by touch.

ACTIVITIES

The text and *beyond*

Comprehension check

1 Chapter 8 is very exciting. Each piece of text below describes a dramatic moment.

1 'There was a noise in the bushes. I saw three figures — Morlocks!'
2 'There were clearly several Morlocks and they were getting nearer.'
3 'Suddenly afraid, I bent down. She was hardly breathing.'
4 'The wood behind us seemed full of the movement of a great crowd.'

Choose four more dramatic pieces from the text. Choose the MOST dramatic.

5 ....
6 ....
7 ....
8 ....

Show your choices to other students. VOTE to decide the most dramatic from 1-8.

2 The table shows five places on the Traveller and Weena's journey. Mark the places where the moments (1-8) in Activity 1 happened. Write the moment below the place. *1* has been done for you.

Porcelain Palace	Bushes	Beginning of the wood	Middle of the wood	Open space
	1			

94

ACTIVITIES

If we stayed here, the Morlocks would kill us.

The Time Traveller has already decided **not** to stay, so he is thinking about an **unreal** situation. We can use the second conditional to talk about **unreal** situations:

if + **past verb**, + *would* + **verb**

Grammar: talking about unreal situations

3 Imagine being lost in the world of 802701. Discuss what you would do in these situations.

0 The Morlocks surround you.
   I would make a fire and drive them away.
1 You find an old gun in the museum.
2 You look down a well and see the Time Machine.
3 Weena wants you to stay in her world forever.
4 The Morlocks want you to leave the Eloi and join them underground.
5 You have a camera with you.
6 You find gold and diamonds in one of the ruins.

Now write second conditional sentences based on the situations (1-6).

0 *If the Morlocks* **surrounded** *me, I* **would make** *a fire.*

Vocabulary: public buildings

4 Complete the sentences (1-8) in the same way as this example.

0 A museum is a place where *you go to look at interesting things from the past.*
1 A stadium is a place where ....
2 An art gallery ....
3 A library ....
4 A police station ....
5 A theatre ....
6 A concert hall ....
7 A shopping mall ....
8 A hospital ....

ACTIVITIES

5 The Traveller finds some things to use as weapons to defend himself against the Morlocks in the ruined museum. What might he find in the places (1-8) in Activity 4?

He might find **a baseball bat** and **a floodlight** in a **stadium**.

Writing

6 PRELIMINARY This is part of a letter you receive from a penfriend.

> I've been reading *The Thirty-Nine Steps*. It's about an innocent man running away from the police and trying to find the real criminals. I love adventure stories and I love hearing about other people's favourite books. Can you tell me about an exciting story that you've read?

Reply to this letter in about 100 words. You can tell the story of Chapter 8 in your own words or choose a story from another book.

Vocabulary: feelings

7 Match some of the feelings with the events. How many of these did you feel when you were reading Chapter 8?

Feelings: amusement   anger   anxiety   fear   happiness   hope   relief   sadness   surprise   sympathy for the Morlocks

Events:
- the Traveller and Weena dance
- they go into the wood
- the Morlocks attack the Traveller
- the fire suddenly spreads
- the Morlocks are blinded and on fire
- Weena dies
- the Traveller is safe

Do you agree with this opinion? *'The best stories create a mixture of many emotions in the readers.'*

ACTIVITIES

Before you read

Predicting the story

1 Which predictions (1-6) do you think are most likely? Choose two. Later, compare your choices with the events of Chapter 9 as you read.

1 The Morlocks will destroy the Time Machine.
2 The Morlocks will allow the Time Traveller inside the Sphinx.
3 The Traveller will find the Time Machine inside the Sphinx.
4 The Traveller will return to the present and live happily.
5 The Traveller will go on a new journey through Time.
6 Nobody will believe his story and he loses his friends.

Vocabulary

2 Complete the paragraph with the words in the box. Use a dictionary, if necessary.

> butterfly   claws   crabs   desert   sand   strike   twilight   wings

THE WORLD AT THE END OF TIME

The sun has gone down but it is not yet night. It is (1) ....
The whole world is a (2) .... , covered in black
(3) .... The only living creatures are huge red
(4) .... that have sharp (5) .... that could
kill a man with one (6) .... Suddenly, a white
(7) .... with huge (8) .... flies through
the air and lands on a red rock.

When you read Chapter 9, see if this paragraph is the same as H.G. Wells's description of the 'world at the end of time'. What similarities and differences are there?

CHAPTER **9**

The journey continues

'**A**s I walked over the smoking ground, I felt in my pockets. I discovered some loose matches that had fallen from the box before the Morlocks took it. I had the weapon of light.

About nine o'clock I reached the hill which I had first climbed. There were the same magnificent palaces and ruins, the same flowering bushes, the silver river, the little people in their colourful clothes. They danced and talked. Some were bathing in the same place as Weena had bathed. I felt sad. I saw also the wells that led to the Under-World. The Eloi were like farm animals, happy during the day but going to a horrible end during the Dark Nights.

I was sad for the human race. Once, there had been the perfect society, safe and healthy. The rich people had enjoyed their pleasures and the workers had enjoyed their jobs. There had been no problem of unemployment or social disturbance.

The journey continues

But intelligence depends on change and danger. It develops to solve problems. I imagine that the Upper-Worlders became useless and pretty without knowing it while the Under-Worlders became heartless like the machines they worked with. But when the Morlocks needed food, they broke old laws against eating other human beings. This is how I explained the world of 802701.

After the terrors of the past days, I slept in the warm sunshine. I woke a little before sunset and came down the hill towards the White Sphinx. I had my iron bar in one hand and the fingers of the other played with the matches in my pocket.

Something completely unexpected waited for me. The bronze doors were open! I paused in surprise. Inside was a small apartment with the Time Machine in a corner. I threw my iron bar to the ground. I didn't need to break into the pedestal. I realised that this was the Morlocks' trap for me. I stepped inside, almost laughing, and went up to the machine. It was cleaned and oiled. Perhaps they had taken it partly to pieces, trying to understand it.

The thing which I expected happened. The bronze doors closed. I was in the dark. I heard them coming towards me. I tried to light the match. It didn't work! It was the type of match that I needed to strike on the box before it would light. I hadn't realised that.

I had the levers with me. Once I had fitted them back onto the Time Machine I could leave. But the Morlocks were close. I swung the levers into the darkness and began to climb onto the seat of the machine. One hand clutched me, then another. They almost took one of the levers from me. I had to butt[1] a Morlock with my head to drive him away. It was a worse fight than in the forest. But

---

1. **butt**: hit with the head, like a goat.

CHAPTER 9

at last I fixed the levers in position. The hands slipped from me. I entered a grey light. I was travelling in Time.

I was sick and confused by the journey. I clung to the machine, only half-seated on it. When I looked at the controls, I was amazed to see that I was travelling, not back to this time but forward, further into the future! Thousands of years passed in seconds.

As I drove on, changes became clear. Days and nights grew longer. They lasted for centuries. Then there was endless twilight.[2] The sun stayed in the west, growing wider and redder. It was a huge, round object shining with heat. I realised that the planet rested; one side of the Earth now faced the sun all the time. Very carefully, I slowed down the Time Machine until I stopped on a great beach.

The sky was no longer blue. It was black in one direction, it was deep red above my head and it was orange-red in the south-east where the sun lay red and motionless, like a ship on the horizon.

The sea had no waves. There was no wind and the air was very thin. A layer of pink salt edged the water. I heard a harsh scream and a thing like a huge white butterfly flew up into the sky and disappeared. Its voice was so sad that I shivered. I looked around and saw that a red rock was moving slowly towards me. It was really a giant crab.[3] Its mouth opened and shut.

I felt something touch my cheek. It was the antenna of another huge crab behind me. Its great claws reached towards me. I held the levers of the Time Machine tightly and escaped into the next month. When I stopped, more huge crabs were on the beach.

---

2. **twilight** : a half-light between day and night.

3. **crab** :

The journey continues

It was a terrible scene: the red eastern sky, the blackness in the north, the dead sea, the hungry monsters. I moved on into the future, stopping every thousand years, exploring the mystery of the Earth's future. The sun grew larger but less bright until, thirty million years in the future, it occupied a tenth of the sky. The beach was lifeless and covered in snow. There was ice along the edge of the sea. There seemed to be no animals. The stars were very bright and still. A black disc moved across the sun. An unknown planet, not the moon, darkened the face of it.

Cold winds blew and the snow grew thicker. No sheep, no birds, no insects. The sun disappeared completely. The sky was black.

I felt horror. The cold was terrible and I breathed with great difficulty. Then the curved edge of the sun re-appeared. I got off the machine to recover but now I saw a black thing moving towards me. Before it could reach me, I managed to climb onto the Time Machine and press the levers.

So I came back. As I travelled, the sun became golden and the sky became blue. I breathed more easily. I saw shadows of buildings. I began to recognise our own architecture as the dials turned towards zero. I saw the walls of my laboratory.

I saw Mrs Watchett, just as I had seen her at the beginning of my journey, but moving in reverse. She disappeared backwards through the door. Then I stopped the machine.

I got off and sat on my chair. I was in my familiar workroom. Had it all been a dream? Not exactly. The machine had started from the south-east corner of the laboratory. Now it was in the north-west corner. It was the distance that the Morlocks had moved it from the little lawn to the pedestal of the Sphinx.

When I came through the hall, I saw a newspaper and read the date. The clock told me it was almost eight o'clock. I heard your

CHAPTER 9

voices and the sounds of dinner. Then I smelt the food and opened the door and saw you all.

This must seem incredible to you. To me, it is incredible that I am here in this room, telling you about my strange adventures. I cannot expect you to believe it. Think of it as a lie or a dream or a prophecy.[4] Perhaps it is a story I have made out of my ideas about the human story. If it is a story, what do you think of it?'

* * *

He stopped speaking and smoked his pipe. I took my eyes off the Time Traveller's face and looked around. The doctor was still looking at him. The journalist looked at his watch. The others were motionless.

The editor said, 'If I were you, I would write novels. You have a great imagination. But I don't believe a word of your story.'

'I hardly believe in it myself. And yet ...' He looked at the flowers on the table and at the damaged skin on his hands.

The doctor examined the flowers. 'They are strange. I don't recognise them. Where did you really get them?'

The Time Traveller put his head in his hands. 'Weena put them in my pocket, when I travelled into Time. Or did she? Was it all a dream?'

He hurried down the hall and into the laboratory. There was the machine. It had dirt on it, a bent rail and grass on the lower parts.

'Yes, it was true,' the Time Traveller said.

We all left by taxi after that.

'It's a huge lie,' the editor said.

I wasn't sure. He had told us about it seriously and calmly.

Next day, I visited the Traveller again. He wasn't in his room, so I went into the laboratory and studied the machine. When I

---

4. **prophecy** : forecast of the future.

CHAPTER 9

touched it, it flickered like a flame. He appeared in the corridor with a small camera and a bag. 'I'm terribly busy,' he said.

'Do you really travel through Time?' I asked.

'I truly do. Look, wait for me in the dining room. Let's have lunch later and I'll prove everything.'

I sat down and read a newspaper. I had an appointment at two o'clock, so after some time I went to say goodbye to him. As I opened the door of the laboratory, I heard strange sounds. A blast of air hit me. I seemed to see a ghostly figure sitting in a moving metal chair. I was able to see through him to the wall beyond. Then, the Time Traveller and the machine had gone.

I was amazed. His servant came to join me and told me he had not gone out of the house since I had arrived. He must be in the future or the past.

I stayed in the house, waiting for an even stranger story. But he didn't appear for lunch. The Time Traveller vanished three years ago. And as everyone knows, he has never returned.

* * *

Will he ever return? Has he gone into the past, to the time of the dinosaurs? Or is he in a nearer future than he found before, at the height of civilisation? He himself had always thought that the future of humanity [5] was negative. Civilisation led nowhere. If he is right, we must try to forget it and live positively. For my comfort, I have beside me two strange white flowers. They seem to tell me that even after humanity becomes weak and unintelligent, gratitude and tenderness will remain in our hearts.

---

5. **humanity** : people.

ACTIVITIES

The text and *beyond*

Comprehension check

1 Give answers to these questions about Chapter 9.

1. Where did the Traveller find the Time Machine?
2. Why did the Morlocks open the doors?
3. What unexpected problem did the Time Traveller have?
4. What dangers did he meet in the far future?
5. What evidence for his time travel did he bring back?
6. Where is the Time Traveller now?
7. Is H.G. Wells's view of the future in this book optimistic[1] or pessimistic?[2]

Interpretation

2 What about you? Look at the sentences (1-8) and rate each one:

5 = probable   4 = possible   3 = maybe   2 = unlikely
1 = this will never happen

1. People will become more intelligent.
2. We will discover ways to remove most diseases.
3. People will create beautiful cities on other planets.
4. People will learn to live in peace.
5. People will destroy the planet.
6. There will be no green spaces in the future.
7. The ice will melt and cities will disappear.
8. There will always be wars.

Add your numbers for 1-4 and 5-8. Compare them with other students' totals. Who is the most optimistic (highest total for 1-4) and the most pessimistic (highest for 5-8)?
Discuss these and other ideas about the future.

---

1. **optimistic**: expecting good things.
2. **pessimistic**: expecting a negative future.

105

ACTIVITIES

If I were you, I would write novels.

> In second conditional sentences, we say **If I were / If he/she were** instead of using *was*.
> NOTE: in informal situations, you may often hear people say **If I was / If he/she was** ... .
>
> **If I were** the Time Traveller,   I'd go back into the past.
> I'd stay in the present.
> I wouldn't time travel any more.

Grammar: *If I were* ...

3 Complete the sentences (1-7) with your own ideas.

1. If I were Superman/Superwoman, ...
2. If I were President of my country, ...
3. If I were a teacher, ...
4. If my parents were ....
5. If I were a top footballer, ...
6. If I were a billionaire, ...
7. If I were ....

T: GRADE 6

Speaking: travel

4 You cannot travel in Time but there are still plenty of wonderful places to visit in the present. Work with another student, asking and answering these questions about travel.

1. Have you travelled to other countries? Tell me about one of your trips.
2. How do you prefer to travel? By plane, train, car? Why?
3. Do you prefer beach holidays, city holidays or countryside holidays? Why?
4. Where would you like to go for your next holiday? Why?
5. Does travelling help to educate people?
6. Is there a difference between a tourist and a traveller?
7. If tourist trips to Mars become a reality, will you go?

ACTIVITIES

Listening

5 Listen to the conversation. Complete the table with the words you hear.

track 13

PAUL	SAM
I'd go back to (0) ...Egypt... .	I'd go back to (4) ....
I'd meet (1)	I'd meet (5) ....
I'd ask: (2) .... did they (3) .... the Pyramids?	I'd ask: (6) .... did you (7) .... after the French revolution?
Then I'd like to meet (8)	Then I'd like to meet (11) ....
I'd ask: How did you (9) .... alone in the (10) .... ?	I'd ask: (12) .... afraid of (13) .... ?
I'd go forward to the year (14)	I'd ask them about the (17) ....
I'd ask: What do you think about (15) .... of the (16) .... ?	I'd ask: Is it (18) .... than it used to be?

Writing and speaking

6 Write the names of six people from the past that you'd like to visit. For each one, write a question that you'd like to ask. Then write a question to ask someone from the future, for example the first person to land on Mars.

	PEOPLE	QUESTIONS
1	....	.... ?
2	....	.... ?
3	....	.... ?
4	....	.... ?
5	....	.... ?
6	....	.... ?

Show your ideas to another student. Discuss the possible answers to all your questions.

107

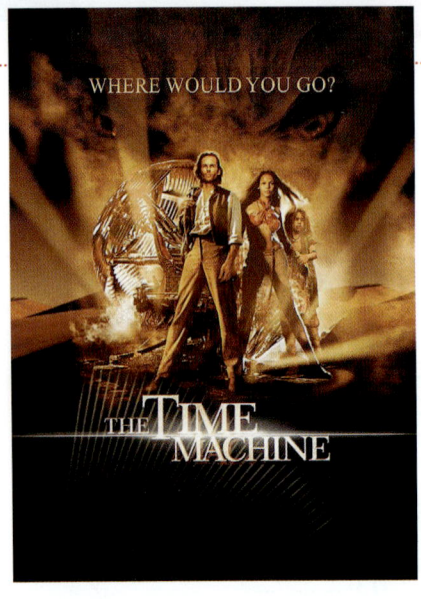

The Time Machine

There has been more than one film of *The Time Machine*, but each time, there have been changes to the original story. In the 1960 American film, the Time Traveller is given a name: H. George Wells. The author becomes a part of the film.

The film begins in a similar way to the book, with the Time Traveller arriving back while his friends are having dinner. However, there are several differences in the way that the story develops.

- First of all, the Traveller goes only a short way into the future and discovers that his friend, Filby, is killed in the First World War. He meets Filby's son.
- He also sees the Second World War. In a later time period, the 1960s, there is a nuclear war [1] which leads to a volcanic eruption. [2]
- The nuclear war leads to the division between the Eloi and the Morlocks.
- There is a more positive relationship between the Traveller and Weena.
- The Traveller encourages the Eloi to fight the Morlocks and win their freedom.

---

1. **nuclear war**: a war which uses atomic weapons.

2. **volcanic eruption**: when a volcano explodes.

The film, directed by George Pal, was successful and won an Oscar for the techniques which it used to represent the journey through Time.

Comprehension check

1. Answer these questions about the films of *The Time Machine*.

   1 In the 1960 film, which 20th-century wars does the Traveller see?
   2 In this film, do the Eloi play a more active role than in the book?
   3 Was the 1960 film a success?
   4 What changes would you make if you were the director?
   5 By using the Internet, what information can you find about:
      a the 2002 film of *The Time Machine*?
      b Simon Wells?
      c other films of H.G. Wells's novels?
      d the Time-Turner?
      e the Time Displacement Sphere?

AFTER READING

Comprehension check

1 Place these events (a-j) in order of time by numbering them 1 to 10, from the earliest (1) to the last (10).

a The Time Traveller rescues Weena. ☐
b He escapes from a giant crab. ☐
c He wakes to find himself surrounded by Morlocks. ☐
d He shows his friends the Time Machine. ☐
e Many Morlocks die in the fire. ☐
f He goes down into the underground. ☐
g He dances with Weena. ☐
h Weena puts a flower in his pocket. ☐
i He lights a fire to prevent the Morlocks following. ☐
j He realises that the Morlocks use the Eloi as food. ☐

Where would you place this event? What is the problem?

k The Time Traveller returns from the future. ☐

2 Answer these questions.

1 What is the first amazing thing which the Traveller does?
2 How does he feel during his journey in the Time Machine?
3 What do the little people eat?
4 Why does Weena follow the Time Traveller everywhere?
5 What does the Time Traveller take from the Porcelain Palace?
6 Why do you think the Morlocks attack the Time Traveller?
7 What happens to the sun in the far future?

3 Speak in favour of the Eloi and/or the Morlocks.

Eloi: We don't harm anyone. You catch us and eat us.
Morlocks: You do not work. We allow you to live beautiful lives.

AFTER READING

4 As the Time Traveller stays longer in the world of 802701, he understands more. He develops three theories about the society.

THEORY 1: Humans have become weak, lazy, pleasure-loving and unintelligent.

THEORY 2: Human beings have separated into two species. The Eloi's happy lifestyle depends on the work of the Morlocks, their slaves. The Eloi are the powerful ones.

THEORY 3: The Morlocks are more powerful than the Eloi; they support them in the same way as farmers look after cows or sheep.

He imagines different reasons for each theory. Which theories do (a-f) support?

a industry developed underground
b lack of competition
c there is no danger in their perfect world
d the Morlocks needed food
e the rich and the workers had separate lives
f the Morlocks are stronger

Themes

5 How are the ideas (1-4) below important in *The Time Machine*? Suggest at least one more theme.

1 The future development of the human race.
2 The power of science.
3 The dangers of division in our society.
4 Time.
5 ....

Are these ideas still relevant to our lives NOW?

Vocabulary

6 Rearrange the letters to find words which are important in the story.

1 VLERE
2 CLORINEAP
3 ELFMA
4 OWNAPE
5 GNUOUDRENRD
6 AHOMPRC
7 TUFEUR
8 ALEAPC
9 PSXNIH
10 BDDLNEI

This reader uses the expansive reading approach: where reading is not only the enjoyment of the story and the discovery of a new language, but an opportunity to make cultural connections.

The new language introduced in this step of our **Reading & Training** series is listed below and language from lower steps is included too. For a complete list for all six steps, see *The Black Cat Graded Readers Handbook* at *blackcat-cideb.com*.

Step Three B1.2

Verb tenses
Present Perfect Simple: unfinished past with *for* or *since* (duration form)
Past Perfect Simple: narrative

Verb forms and patterns
Regular verbs and all irregular verbs in current English
Causative: *have / get* + object + past participle
Reported questions and orders with *ask* and *tell*

Modal verbs
Would: hypothesis
Would rather: preference
Should (present and future reference): moral obligation
Ought to (present and future reference): moral obligation
Used to: past habits and states

Types of clause
2nd conditional: *if* + past, *would(n't)*
Zero, 1st and 2nd conditionals with *unless*
Non-defining relative clauses with *who* and *where*
Clauses of result: *so; so ... that; such ... that*
Clauses of concession: *although, though*

Other
Comparison: *(not) as / so ... as; (not) ... enough to; too ... to*

Step Three
If you enjoyed this reader, try another one in Step Three...

- *Rain, Rain, Go Away!* by Nicola Prentis
- *Great Mysteries of Our World* by Gina D. B. Clemen
- *Twelfth Night* by William Shakespeare

Step Four
...or take a step forward to Step Four!

- *American Horror* by Edgar Allan Poe
- *Dracula* by Bram Stoker
- *The Moonstone* by Wilkie Collins